We Will
Prove Them
Herewith

We Will Prove Them Herewith

Neal A. Maxwell

Deseret Book Company
Salt Lake City, Utah

© 1982 Deseret Book Company
All rights reserved
Printed in the United States of America
First printing March 1982

Library of Congress Cataloging in Publication Data

Maxwell, Neal A.
    We will prove them herewith.

    Includes index.
    1. Christian life—Mormon authors. I. Title.
BX8656.M386   248.4'8933   82-1532
ISBN 0-87747-912-7   AACR2

To President Spencer W. Kimball, who so demonstrably epitomizes the virtues discussed in this book, especially "unwearied diligence" and "enduring well to the end"—with everlasting admiration and love, and with appreciation that the Lord's calls to the author to the ranks of the General Authorities in 1974 and to the Twelve in 1981 came through this remarkable twelfth prophet of this dispensation.

Contents

Acknowledgments

The author expresses appreciation, once again, to those who have helped move this latest literary enterprise along:

To Jeananne Hornbarger for her patient and faithful assistance in the preparation of the manuscript; to President Bruce Hafen, Elizabeth Haglund, Dr. Sears Evans, Dr. Roy W. Doxey, and James Jardine for their suggestions and insights in the refining of the draft that was placed before them; to Grant Anderson in the Church Historical Library, who has been helpful in retrieving some of the illuminating quotations of church leaders that are used herein; and once again to Dr. Lowell M. Durham, Jr., who has offered encouragement, and to Eleanor Knowles, who has done her usual fine job of editing.

Introduction

The Lord has described His plan of redemption as the plan of happiness. (Alma 42:8, 16.) Yet none of us is likely to be a stranger to sorrow.

Conversationally, we reference this great design almost too casually at times; we even sketch its rude outlines on chalkboards and paper as if it were the floor plan for an addition to one's house. However, when we really take time to ponder the plan, it is breathtaking and overpowering. Indeed, one cannot decide which creates the most awe—its very vastness or its intricate, individualized detail.

The vastness of it all is truly overwhelming. We are living on a small planet that is part of a very modest solar system, which, in turn, is located at the outer edge of the awesome Milky Way galaxy. If we were sufficiently distant from the Milky Way, it would be but another bright dot among countless other bright dots in space, all of which could cause us to conclude, comparatively, "that man is nothing." (Moses 1:10.)

Yet we are rescued by reassuring realities such as that God knows and loves each of us, personally and perfectly. Hence, there is incredible intimacy in the vastness of it all. Are not the very hairs of one's head numbered? Is not the fall of each sparrow noticed? (Matthew 10:29-30.) Has Jesus not borne, and therefore knows, our individual sins, sicknesses, and infirmities? (Alma 7:11-12.)

Furthermore, the eventual purpose of it all is centered on us—"to bring to pass the immortality and eternal life of man." (Moses 1:39.) President Brigham Young said there are millions of earths like this one so that, as Isaiah said, certain planets can be inhabited (Isaiah 45:18) as God's plan of salvation is executed and reexecuted. Truly, as the Psalmist said, "We are the people of his pasture, and the sheep of his hand." (Psalm 95:7.) How glorious is our God!

Not only has He told us that His "course is one eternal round" (D&C 3:2), but are we not also given intriguing intimations such as how planets "move in their times and their seasons" and how "all these kingdoms, and the inhabitants thereof" are to know the joy of seeing the countenance of the Lord—"every kingdom in its hour, and in its time, and in its season"? (See D&C 88:42, 61.)

Has not the Almighty God who oversees it all shared with us almost more than we can comprehend about His work?

We, individually and collectively, are at the very center of God's purposes. Since God is so serious about our joy, can we be less than serious? Can we safely postpone striving to become like Him? Since there can be no true joy for us apart from doing His work, can we risk being diverted by other chores? Dare we stop short of enduring well to the end? Can we not be thankful for a purposeful life even when we have a seemingly purposeless day? Should we not be grateful for God's plan for us even when our own plans for ourselves go awry?

Of course, this grand plan and design for our happiness is not something that exists merely to strike awe in us or to evoke gasps of gladness. It does not exist apart from us, but involves us—painfully at times and happily at other times, but relentlessly always.

The implications for this, our second estate, are many once we realize this life is (1) a divinely designated proving ground (Abraham 3:25), (2) a circumstance in which those who triumph overcome by faith that is deliberately tried (D&C 76:53), and (3) an unusual environment featuring, among other things, a dimension called time (Alma 40:8).

It seems clear, not only scripturally but logically, that this second estate could not include either the direct memories or the reference experiences of our first estate. If such were to impinge overmuch upon this second estate, our mortality would not be a true proving ground.

In like manner, the veil also stands between us and that which lies ahead, our third and everlasting estate. If, for instance, our association with resurrected beings in this second estate were the order of the day, if they walked with us in the marketplace and conversed with us in the gospel doctrine class, no true growth or test as was envisioned could really occur.

Much, therefore, as we might like to have the curtains parted so that not only "on a clear day," but all the time, we could see forever, thereby knowing the circumstances, events, and challenges that lie ahead of us—those things are, for the most part, kept carefully from us. Indeed, it appears that such understanding is usually given only to those individuals who have progressed sufficiently, spiritually, that they can be trusted with such knowledge, because it will not distract or divert them or cause them to slacken. To give people spiritual knowledge in advance of their capacity to understand it or to apply it is no favor.

Even yesterday's righteous experience does not guarantee us against tomorrow's relapse. A few who have had supernal spiritual experiences have later fallen. Hence, enduring well to the end assumes real significance, and we are at risk till the end!

While there is a spiritual ecology (and when we violate it we pay a certain price), the costs or consequences are not always immediate nor externally visible. Thieves are not always brought immediately to justice. A child-abusing parent is not at once restrained. So, in a hundred ways that could be illustrated, the outward judgment of God does not immediately fall upon an erring individual in order that this second estate could be a true proving ground; and, mercifully, so we can, if we will, know the refreshment of renewal and repentance. Without repentance, the past would forever hold the future hostage.

Since, for example, almost all individuals have a tendency to abuse power and authority—not just a few, not even a mere majority—how are the relevant lessons about the righteous use of power to be learned except in this laboratory setting? Could we have truly experienced the risks and opportunities of power merely by attending some pointed lectures or doing some directed reading during our first estate? Was it not necessary to experience, "according to the flesh," what it is like to be on the receiving end of unrighteous dominion? And the necessity of repentance when one has been on the giving end? The very absence, for instance, on the human political scene of attributes such as genuine humility, mercy, and meekness is a grim reminder about how essential these qualities are to the governance of self or nation.

In some respects, it is easier to govern a whole people than oneself. Of one ancient political leader it is candidly recorded: "And he did do justice unto the people, but not unto himself because of his many whoredoms; wherefore he was cut off from the presence of the Lord." (Ether 10:11.) One can cater to mortal constituencies but lose the support of the one Elector who matters!

We know that God's "word of power" brings entire new worlds into being and causes others to pass away. (Moses 1:35-38.) But the powers of heaven cannot be handled or controlled except upon the basis of righteousness. (D&C 121:36.) Real righteousness cannot, therefore, be a superficial, ritualistic thing. It must arise from the deepest convictions of the soul, not from a desire merely to "go along" with the Heavenly Regime simply because that's how things are done. God's power, unlike mortal power, is accessed only by those who have developed, to a requisite degree, God's attributes.

Jesus counseled us, too, concerning materialism and "the deceitfulness of riches" (Matthew 13:22) and how hard it is for those who trust in riches to enter into the kingdom of God (Luke 18:24). Another of those scalding but divine generalizations! The relevant mortal experiences permit, but do not guarantee, that we will learn about what should come first in life. Can those who are diverted by riches or the search for riches and thus fail to discern the real purposes of life be safely trusted with greater dominions that call for even greater discernment? "And he that overcometh, and keepeth my works unto the end, to him will I give power over the nations." (Revelation 2:26.)

Could we truly appreciate the supremacy of spiritual things without experiencing the limitations of materialism? Not in just one brief encounter, but day by day?

Since "he that hath no rule over his own spirit is like a city that is broken down, and without walls" (Proverbs 25:28), how could we develop and test our capacity to govern ourselves without the specific opportunities for growth and failure that daily life affords? In fact, is not managing life's little challenges so often the big challenge? Those who wait for a single, spectacular, final exam are apt to fail the daily quizzes!

We are to strive to become perfect even as our Father in heaven is perfect. But this is not just generalized goodness; rather, it is the attainment of specific attributes. (Matthew 5:48.)

So it is that, if God intends to use us (and He does), He must school us so that we are emulating His attributes and functioning in harmony with the laws of His universe while yet in this "proving ground" setting.

Moreover, even when we fail to develop an eternal attribute sufficiently, our mortal experiences will nevertheless have shown us just how precious that attribute is. How much easier, later on, to accept with appreciation the righteous dominion of those who have so progressed. Again, could such appreciation and acceptance have been generated in the abstract?

We are even reassured that our mortal performance will be judged according to what has been allotted to us and how we use our talents within that allocation. (See Alma 29:3, 6; Matthew 25:14-30.) We will not be able to invoke, justifiably, either deprivational or circumstantial evidence in our own behalf later on to show that we were dealt with unjustly. The record will be clear. Perhaps that stark reality will contribute to the response of those who, at judgment time, will wish to be buried under mountains and rocks to hide them from the face of God! (See Revelation 6:16.)

Thus the whole mortal schooling process has been so carefully structured in order to achieve results that could be achieved in no other way. (Helaman 5:9.) We can come to know the Lord as our loving, tutoring Father and God—but not as a policeman posted at every intersection of our lives!

Hence our submissiveness to the Lord must be real, not the equivalent of obeying the speed limit only as long as the highway patrolman is there in his pace-car. Indeed, awaiting full development is our willingness "to submit to all things which the Lord seeth fit to inflict upon [us], even as a child doth submit to his father." (Mosiah 3:19.) This is a sobering gospel truth about submissiveness. It is a wintry declaration with icy implications. This truth is not one likely to evoke from us an "Oh, goodie" response!

During our mortal schooling in submissiveness, we will see the visible crosses that some carry, but other crosses will go unseen. A few individuals may appear to have no trials at all, which, if it were so, would be a trial in itself. Indeed, if, as do trees, our souls had rings to measure the years of greatest personal growth, the wide rings would likely reflect the years of greatest moisture—but from tears, not rainfall.

Most of our suffering comes from sin and stupidity; it is very real, and, nevertheless, growth can still occur with real repentance. But the highest form of suffering appears to be reserved for the innocent who undergo tutorial training.

Thus we see how gospel truths concerning the plan of salvation are much more than a "tourist guide" for the second estate; they include a degree of understanding of what Paul called "the deep things of God." (1 Corinthians 2:10.) In our moments of deep anguish, suffering, and bewilderment, in those moments when we ask in faith for certain outcomes and are refused, because to give them to us would not be right (3 Nephi 18:20), then our faith is either deepened or slackened.

Yes, even in our prayers we can, unintentionally, ask "amiss." (2 Nephi 4:35.) No wonder humility is such an everlasting virtue. For us to accept God's "no" as an affirmative indication of His love rather than a lack thereof and as a signal that we have asked amiss— this is truly humility.

How often have you and I in our provincialism prayed to see ahead and, mercifully, been refused, lest our view of the present be blurred?

How many times have we been blessed by *not* having our prayers answered, at least according to the specifications set forth in our petitions?

How many times have frustrating, even grueling, experiences from which we have sought relief turned out later to have been part of a necessary preparation that led to much more happiness? "And now when Alma heard this, . . . he beheld that their afflictions had truly humbled them and that they were *in a preparation to hear* the word." (Alma 32:6. Italics added.)

How many times have we impatiently expressed our discontent with seemingly ordinary and routine circumstances that were divinely designed, shaping circumstances for which, later on, we were very grateful? Alas, have there perhaps not also been those times when we have been grumpy with God or, unlike Job, even "charged God foolishly"? (Job 1:22.) How many times, naively and ungraciously, have we vigorously protested while on our way to a blessing?

Thus it is that our faith and trust in our Heavenly Father, so far as this mortal experience is concerned, consists not simply of faith and gladness that He exists, but is also a faith and trust that, if we are humble, He will tutor us, aiding our acquisition of needed attributes and experiences while we are in mortality. We trust not only the Designer but also His design of life itself, including our portion thereof!

Our response to the realities of the plan should not be resignation or shoulder-shrugging fatalism, but reverential acceptance. If at times we wonder, we should know what it is to be filled with wonderment. Why should it surprise us that life's most demanding tests as well as life's most significant opportunities for growth in life usually occur within marriage and the family? How can revolving door relationships, by contrast, be a real test of our capacity to love? Is being courteous to the stranger on the bus as difficult as being courteous to a family member who is competing for the bathroom morning after morning? Does fleeting disappointment with a fellow office worker compare to the betrayal of a spouse? Does a raise in pay even approach the lift we receive from rich family life?

Besides, even the most seemingly ordinary life contains more than enough clinical opportunities for our personal growth and development. By the way, while mortality features "an opposition in all things" (2 Nephi 2:15), we need feel no obligation to supply opposition or to make life difficult. Sufficient unto each situation are the challenges thereof.

Should it surprise us that in striving to acquire and develop celestial attributes, the greater the interpersonal proximity, the greater the challenge? Is not patience, for instance, best developed among those with whom we interface incessantly? The same is true with any of the other eternal attributes. Hence the high adventure of marriage and family life—and why it is that in our time so many run away from these challenges thinking they can avoid having to confront themselves by losing themselves in other endeavors or life-styles.

And when the gossamer veil called time is too much with us, let us recall that ere long time will be no more. Time is measured only to man anyway. (See Revelation 10:6; Alma 40:8; D&C 84:100.) Meanwhile, let us make allowance for the rapidity with which time seems to pass especially when we are happy. Jacob found it so: "And Jacob served seven years for Rachel; and they seemed unto him but a few days, for the love he had to her." (Genesis 29:20.) On such a scale, each of us has but "a few days" left in mortality.

As men or women of Christ, we can be led by Him through this second estate; in the words of Helaman, "in a straight and narrow course across that everlasting gulf of misery which is prepared to engulf the wicked—and land their souls, yea, their immortal souls, at the right hand of God in the kingdom of heaven, to sit down with Abraham, and Isaac, and with Jacob, and with all our holy fathers, to go no more out." (Helaman 3:29-30.)

"To go no more out." An intriguing promise! For the busy, for those ceaselessly on the move, for the homeless, for the lonely, and for widows and widowers—and for others of us who will become such— does not the prospect of this homecoming in such grand and everlasting circumstances warm the soul? Not, of course, that life hereafter is to consist of unending repose; rather, for those who attain the presence of God "to go no more out," nowhere is really "out," and now is forever. As time is no more, likewise space will shrink irrevocably. For all we know, the speed of light may prove to be too slow to do some of what must be done.

No wonder it is called the plan of happiness! No wonder we must earnestly strive to become "grounded, rooted, established, and settled"!

Since we are part of the Lord's unfolding purposes, we would do well to remember how deep Divine determination really is: "There is nothing that the Lord thy God shall take in his heart to do but what he shall do it." (Abraham 3:17.) Having so very long ago set in motion His plan of salvation, God will not revise the structure or the schedule of this second estate just because you and I have a bad day.

It is especially helpful to remember, therefore, that the temptations and challenges we face in mortality are common to man. (1 Corinthians 10:13.) Yet we must respond uncommonly. Jesus responded uniquely though "suffering pains and afflictions and temptations of every kind." (Alma 7:11.)

It is also useful to ponder the fact that, along with even the Savior Himself, we are to experience certain things "according to the flesh" (Alma 7:12) and, as have the righteous in other times, to learn "in process of time" (Moses 7:21).

Built, therefore, into the seemingly ordinary experiences of life are abundant opportunities for us to acquire the eternal attributes, such as love, mercy, meekness, patience, submissiveness, and to develop and sharpen such skills as how to communicate, motivate, delegate, and manage our talents, time, and thoughts in accordance with eternal priorities. These attributes and skills are portable, are never obsolete; they will be much needed in the next world.

If we ponder just what it is that will rise with us in the resurrection, it seems clear that our intelligence will rise with us, meaning not simply our IQ, but also our capacity to receive and apply truth. Our talents, attributes, and skills will rise with us; certainly also our capacity to learn, our degree of self-discipline, and our capacity to work. Our precise form of work here may have no counterpart there, but the capacity to work will never be obsolete.

To be sure, we cannot, while here, entirely avoid contact with the obsolescent and the irrelevant; it is all around us. But one can be around irrelevancy without becoming attached to it. Certainly we should not become preoccupied with obsolete things, yet we need not have a discontent with the paraphernalia of this probationary estate. Yet to mistake mortal props for the real drama that is underway is a grave error to be avoided.

Keeping our sense of proportion *whatever* we do, keeping our precious perspective *wherever* we are, and keeping the commandments *however* we are tested— these reflect being "settled" in our discipleship.

Becoming grounded, rooted, established, and settled is not easy. Nor is remaining so, for we are crowded by the cares of the world, diverted by the praise of the world, buffeted by the trials of the world, drawn by the appetites and temptations of the world, and bruised by the hardness of the world.

Once established in our "errand from the Lord," we will have the Holy Spirit as our guide and, however we are stretched and tested, the Spirit will keep us vibrant and alive. Things that we had never supposed will come into view. Seeming routine will turn out to be resplendent. Ordinary people will seem quite the opposite. What we once thought to be the humdrum of life will give way to symphonic sounds. Circumstances or a conversation that looks pedestrian will nevertheless cause a quiet moment of personal resolve or a decision that will affect all eternity. Sometimes amid routine we even sense the significance of what is happening, but there will be no headlines or bands playing.

A very significant part of getting settled, therefore, consists of coming to terms with the reality that the seeming routine of life, like trials, can either bring us closer to God or move us away from Him.

What seems commonplace seldom is, and ordinariness is so often a cover for extraordinariness. The laboratory of life only appears to be a quiet and uneventful place. Even so, some let the seeming ordinariness dampen their spirits. Though actually coping and growing, some lack the quiet, inner-soul satisfaction that can steady them. Instead, some experience a lingering sense that there is something more important they should be doing and that their chores are somehow not quite what was expected—as if, for instance, what is quietly achieved in righteous, individual living or in parenthood is not sufficiently spectacular.

Feeling unrequited as to role and feeling underwhelmed do not occur, however, because of a structural failure in the divinely designed second estate; rather, they occur because of a lack of love, for love helps us to see and to respond to those opportunities which have been allotted to us and which lie unused all about us.

Before one complains, therefore, about the curriculum in mortality, or more particularly his current class schedule, he would do well to remember Who designed the curriculum and to allow for however many other places it has been used successfully.

True, there are seeming flat periods in life when we may feel underwhelmed, but in such situations we had best get back to the basics as to why we are here. In the terse communique from the Gods about our being placed on this planet, the basic objective of life on this planet is stated: "And we will prove them herewith, to see if they will do all things whatsoever the Lord their God shall command them." (Abraham 3:25.)

If our focus on this, life's fundamental purpose, is blurred, we will not see "things as they really are." (Jacob 4:13.)

There should be no surprise about how the second estate features lessons to be learned patiently and painfully "according to the flesh." There should be no resentment or mystery regarding our personal development "in process of time." God's purposes are plain!

Furthermore, since we are here to be thus proved, how can that occur except we are tested? If we are here to learn to choose wisely, how can that occur except there be alternatives? If our soul is to be stretched, how can that happen without growing pains? How can personal development really occur amid routine unless we have authentic challenges to practice on?

When life is viewed superficially, granted it can seem routine and pedestrian. However, what appears on the surface can be a thin cover for developments of spiritual significance. Those who passed by the football stadium at the University of Chicago several decades ago did not know what was underway below those empty stadium seats. The atom was being split—after which the world was never again to be the same! Such a quiet stadium, too.

It remains for us in our varied circumstances, but with our common challenges, to make the interplay of our time and talent bring about the development of the key eternal attributes and the everlasting skills.

Any resulting "advantage" we have in the world to come clearly will result from taking advantage of the opportunities this life affords us. Hence those who are *grounded, rooted, established,* and *settled* find real joy in being serious about the eternal objectives on which this life should focus.

When anciently we shouted for joy in anticipation of this mortal experience, we did not then think it would be an ordinary, pedestrian thing at all. We sensed the impending high adventure. Let us be true to that first and more realistic reaction!

So much depends, therefore, upon our maintaining gospel perspective in the midst of ordinariness, the pressures of temptation, tribulation, deprivation, and the cares of the world. As we come to love the Lord more and more, we can understand rather than resent His purposes. Besides, He who should know has said "there is no other way." Furthermore, since there is but one path back to our true home, this wisdom by C.S. Lewis is worth pondering: "Our Father in Heaven refreshes us on the journey through life with some pleasant inns, but he will not encourage us to mistake them for home."

When the Savior urged even His closest disciples to "settle this in your hearts, that ye shall do the things which I shall teach, and command you" (JST, Luke 14:28), He also spoke of the high costs of discipleship "signifying there should not any man follow him, unless he was able to continue" (JST, Luke 14:31). Clearly Jesus was underscoring the importance of having His followers become thoroughly *grounded* in the gospel, *rooted* in resolve, *established* in their expectations about life, and *settled* in their devotion to the Savior.

15

Chapter One

Grounded, Rooted, Established, and Settled

(Ephesians 3:17; 1 Peter 5:10)

Two intriguing but unelaborated-upon verses concerning the gospel seed appear in the Book of Matthew:

"Some fell upon stony places, where they had not much earth: and forthwith they sprung up, because they had *no deepness of earth*:

"And when the *sun was up*, they were *scorched*; and because they had *no root*, they withered away." (Matthew 13:5-6. Italics added.)

Perhaps that is all the Savior said on that occasion. If He said more, the balance is among those "plain and precious things" missing from the Bible. (1 Nephi 13:28.) In Alma, however, we do get an elaboration concerning the gospel seed and how it can subsequently both flourish or wither. (See Alma 32.)

Even if we can do no more "than desire to believe," said Alma, we are to "give place" for the gospel seed; we are to let that desire work within us by trying the experiment of the gospel's goodness in the laboratory of life, giving it place in our thoughts, attitudes, and schedules; otherwise it will be crowded out of its place by other pressing cares.

When it is properly planted, we then experience the seed's swelling growth. We discern its goodness, and our *faith* "in that thing" can eventually be transformed into genuine *knowledge*. Unlike Jonah's gourd, however, it does not grow overnight. Some of its fruit only comes "by and by." Nevertheless, we are responsible for nourishing the sprouting seed; otherwise it will not develop a good root system, and when the heat of the sun comes, it will wither. And how do we nourish it? By "faith, with great diligence, and with patience." (Alma 32.)

How vital it is to be rooted and grounded in order to take the scorching heat that will be a part of that special summer of circumstances which precedes the second coming of the Son of Man in power and glory and majesty. A brief, scorching season, that summer will climax the centuries as the special moment among the millennia of mortal time.

The unnourished and the shallow will not endure, because they cannot stand the heat. They are not likely to acknowledge that as the real reason, however, preferring to find a convenient cause over which to become offended, or wishing to cover behavioral lapses by a supposed grievance. These are they who, among other things, will end up, as my friend James Jardine has observed, "preaching what they practice"!

The gospel glow shining about a righteous individual or a righteous people usually attracts persecution. But this is not the only accompanying sign. Enoch could tell us something about this phenomenon; those in his ancient Zion were resented by some who "stood afar off." Latter-day Saints are not yet a fully worthy people, but even now there is building a visible ring of resentment around Zion today. It includes those who once had a shallow faith but are now critics. Their tree of testimony lacked root; it withered, and they plucked "it up and cast it out," occasionally with great public display. (Alma 32:38.)

In heavy winds, even large pine trees are sometimes unexpectedly blown down, because though they appeared secure, their root systems were very shallow.

People who are grounded in the Lord and His gospel have a deep and extensive root system. Having applied the various principles and truths of the gospel, they have specific faith from and experience with each principle in its turn. Their faith is not a generalized feeling, but reflects specific experience with interlocking principles.

Being settled means that one refuses to be blown or "moved away from the hope of the gospel." (Colossians 1:23.) Neither surrounding secular skepticism nor vexing personal trials unsettle him. This settled condition is not the result of a single sudden act, of course. Nor is it an attainment followed by sweet repose, nor is it a static circumstance. Rather, it is like pounding one's pitons into the rocky and ascending surface of the windswept and sun-scorched straight and narrow path. Because one's pitons are anchored, he can inch forward, ever praying that he might "come off conqueror," led by "the good shepherd" who knows the only way up and through the peaks of this probationary estate. (D&C 10:5; Alma 5:60.) When one is so anchored, he can then avoid the most common and fatal forms of falling away, which Jesus described as *temptation, persecution, tribulation,* and the *cares, riches,* and *pleasures* of this life. (Matthew 13:21; Luke 8:13-14.)

Achieving such spiritual maturity is essential in any age, but especially in our time. The following prophecy of President Brigham Young is but one indicator of the urgent need to "escape the hands of the servants of Satan that do uphold his work," for his network expands: "It was revealed to me in the commencement of this Church, that the Church would spread, prosper, grow and extend, and that *in proportion* to the spread of the Gospel among the nations of the earth, *so would the power of Satan rise.*"[1]

As described by Zephaniah, Church members in the last days live, though blessed with the light of the gospel, in a day of gloominess. (Zephaniah 1:15.) In these times of widespread commotion, disorder, unrest, agitation, and insurrection, the hearts of many will fail. (D&C 45:26; 88:91.) Others will be sorely tried but will, in their extremities, seek succor from seers as did the anxious young man who approached the prophet Elijah as ancient Israel was surrounded: "Alas, my master! how shall we do?" The answer of today's prophets will be the same: "Fear not: for they that be with us are more than they that be with them." Only when we are settled spiritually can we understand that kind of arithmetic. Only then will our eyes, like the young man's, be opened. (2 Kings 6:15-17.)

Then what more shall we do to become grounded, rooted, established, and settled in the face of such stern circumstances?

Though the Church is sometimes criticized for being authoritarian, it wisely places great emphasis upon its members learning to be righteously self-reliant. Having oil in our own lamps, as a matter of fact, entitles us to be partakers of the essential gift of personal revelation. Being settled involves the cultivation of this great gift. President Joseph F. Smith said in 1912:

"The gift of revelation does not belong to one man

solely; it is not a gift that pertains to the Presidency of the Church and the Twelve Apostles alone. It is . . . the right and privilege of every man, every woman, and every child who has reached the years of accountability, to enjoy the spirit of revelation, and to be possessed of the spirit of inspiration in the discharge of their duties as members of the Church. It is the privilege of every individual member of the Church to have revelation for his own guidance, for the direction of his life and conduct."[2]

Surely Father Lehi, who had a revelatory dream, rejoiced when his son Nephi was favored with an elaborating and revelatory dream!

Moses did not resent the spreading of a particular spiritual gift:

"And there ran a young man, and told Moses, and said, Eldad and Medad do prophesy in the camp.

"And Joshua the son of Nun, the servant of Moses, one of his young men, answered and said, My lord Moses, forbid them.

"And Moses said unto him, Enviest thou for my sake? *would God that all the Lord's people were prophets,* and that the Lord would put his spirit upon them!" (Numbers 11:27-29. Italics added.)

Those who are established and settled, among other things, cultivate this immensely important gift of personal revelation.

President Smith even went so far as to say that it was the privilege of each member of the Church "to have it revealed to you whether [the president was] a servant of God or a servant of men." As with the young man who inquired of Elijah, Church members need to know that they can have confidence in today's prophets and seers.

Following inspired prophets is the pattern for

those who are established in their faith. As Elder George A. Smith reportedly told one man who wanted to wait in the East for the impending redemption of Zion, the nearest way to Missouri was through Great Salt Lake City![3] There will be equivalent paradoxes and choices in our lives today.

Vital it is, therefore, that we have oil in our lamps, having taken the Holy Spirit as our guide, in order to be able to follow the prophets and know that we are following the will of the Lord. (D&C 45:57.)

Walter Bagehot wrote, "Conscience is the converting intuition; that which turns me from the world without to that within—from things which are seen to the realities which are not seen."[4] So it is that our very perceptual powers, which determine the degree to which we see "things as they really are," to a large extent are governed by the aliveness of our conscience, which the Holy Spirit sharpens and stimulates.

The Church does not desire blind obedience; rather, that we see things with the eye of faith. (Ether 12:19.) Elder John A. Widtsoe observed: "The doctrine of the Church cannot be fully understood unless it is tested by mind and feelings, by intellect and emotions, by every power of the investigator. . . . There is no place in the Church for blind adherence."[5]

Besides, real obedience is not blind. It reflects the reassurances of previous tutoring experiences from the Lord, inducing us to trust Him and His prophets, again and again. Our love of God is binding, not blinding, love. Being established connotes a continuum in our relationship with God and His prophets. President Brigham Young put it bluntly: "I am more afraid that this people have so much confidence in their leaders that they will not inquire for themselves of God whether they are led by Him. I am fearful they settle down in a state of blind self-security, trusting their eternal destiny in the hands of their leaders with a reckless confidence that in itself would thwart the purposes of God in their salvation, and *weaken that influence they could give to their leaders*, did they know for themselves, by the revelations of Jesus, that they are led in the right way."[6]

Those who are grounded, rooted, and established will not withhold their supportive influence from Church leaders.

Neither will the faithful be deceived, as President Brigham Young promised: "I will say to my brethren and sisters, Were your faith concentrated upon the proper object, your confidence unshaken, your lives pure and holy, every one fulfilling the duties of his or her calling according to the Priesthood and capacity bestowed upon you, you would be *filled with the Holy Ghost*, and it would be as *impossible for any man to deceive and lead you to destruction* as for a feather to remain unconsumed in the midst of intense heat."[7]

Elder Boyd K. Packer said in a sermon on self-reliance that as we solve our own problems, we must do it "in the Lord's own way": "If we are not careful, we can lose the power of individual revelation. . . . Spiritual independence and self-reliance is a sustaining power in the Church. If we rob the members of that, how can they get revelation for themselves? How will they know there is a prophet of God? How can they get answers to prayers? How can they know for *sure* for themselves?"[8]

When we approach our problems in His way, we are guided by His Spirit. Being settled in our discipleship, therefore, requires the successful utilization of the Holy Spirit as our guide both in our decision and as our Comforter. We will need guidance in using our agency, but also deep comfort in coping with the disappointments of the day and in the seasonal sorrows of life.

So much, therefore, of what the Lord's prophets seek to do is to educate us in the perspective of eternity. They do not enjoy *telling* us so much as they wish to *teach* us, ever hoping that the divine perspectives imparted will be used by us as we govern ourselves. Prophets are the last to regret the spreading of true individual inspiration.

It is not merely a matter of *lessening* the burdens of the few, but of *enlarging* perspectives of the many. Moreover, given what there will be to do in the governance of worlds to come, how could we be wisely spared personal experience in the governance of both self and community here?

If life's burdens were too small and too little felt and its choices too easy, how would we—how could we—learn what we need to learn? Moreover, just as prophets desire the spread of legitimate personal revelation, so they, also, desire the sharing of leadership responsibility.

"And many more things did king Mosiah write unto them, unfolding unto them all the trials and troubles of a righteous king, yea, all the travails of soul for their people, and also all the murmurings of the people to their king; and he explained it all unto them.

"And he told them that these things ought not to be; but that *the burden should come upon all the people, that every man might bear his part.*" (Mosiah 29:33-34. Italics added.)

Thus, to choose the "good part" which, as with Mary, will not be taken from us, but likewise, to "bear" our "part," are both vital to our experience in this proving second estate. Little wonder that when a whole people were well taught, as were the people of King Mosiah, "who explained it all unto them," the people "were convinced of the truth of his words," and "they did wax strong in love towards Mosiah; yea, they did esteem him more than any other man." (Mosiah 29:33, 37, 40.) True pupils will always revere a true tutor!

Our experiences in process of time not only help us to compare the bad and the good, but also, when we are established spiritually, we can come not only to abhor but also to understand how sin occurs. Sin, for instance, is often the wrongheaded, twisted, and stupid way of expressing some basic needs that we all have, such as for belonging and recognition. The adversary understands and plays upon these basic needs. Thus this life helps us to know not only the bitter and the sweet, but also the often ironic relationship between the two.

One who seeks riches for riches' sake may be doing so in a mistaken belief that he is achieving security, for riches bring their own insecurity; thieves break in and moths and rust corrupt; stock markets fluctuate and even collapse.

Sexual immorality is sometimes but the despairing side of the search for affectional security and belonging. It brings instead, in the words of Jacob, a profound sadness in which many hearts die "pierced with deep wounds." (Jacob 2:35.) Despair, not the media's depicted delight, is the final feeling. Therefore, individuals who seek to reassure themselves through sexual immorality only lower their self-esteem. Those who thus seek for affectional security get just the opposite: added alienation.

Those who become grounded in the gospel can see

such paradoxes and avoid a most common form of falling away described by Jesus—temptation.

Each of us seeks deserved and legitimate recognition, but a wrong approach can produce an awful addiction, for the passion for preeminence is a dangerous passion. The eternal attribute of meekness helps us to pay no heed to this passion.

All of our legitimate and deepest needs can be met, but only through obedience to the commandments of God. Being grounded, rooted, established, and settled means understanding that central reality.

Besides, is there any recognition greater than His recognition of His faithful followers as His friends? Is there any security to exceed that of living with Him in mansions that He has lovingly prepared for us? Is there any better belonging than being in His presence forever and ever? Is there any greater identity that we can know than being a righteous daughter or righteous son of God? Are there any promises of adventure greater than His assurances to us about wider and everlasting opportunities for service that await us? Is there any better way to overcome loneliness than to lose ourselves in His service? If we are settled, we will possess such perspective, and the heat of the day will not cause us to faint and become disoriented.

Sinners consistently mistake a passing mood for a basic need. Let it be said again: because our basic needs are so natural and powerful, they can be managed *only* by keeping the commandments and by following the straight and narrow way. Try as people may, there is no other path to happiness. Those who walk in their own way often think their path is unique—but all such paths finally converge into that wide way and end at that broad gate which leads to misery and self-destruction.

Hence, when we become settled, we also settle into the correct view that sin is sadness and righteousness is happiness, while those of shallow root who are being scorched will be fevered, faint, and disoriented. The delirium so caused produces its own irrational assertions not unlike those of a physical fever.

Sin is often the search for happiness gone wild—and sometimes even mad! For instance, when, soaked as so many have been in the fashionable selfishness of our time, people announce, "I have a *right* to be happy," they are usually about to do something *wrong*. There is a clear and present danger in one's indulging his fevered feelings of being deprived.

A saint is settled; let the world be in commotion, but he will not be tossed to and fro.

When people fall, they do not suddenly stop believing in the atonement; they simply start believing in their impulses. Their discipline disappears as their perspective shrinks. Irrationality replaces illumination.

The pressures at the moment of temptation are undeniably real, made so by the impulse that becomes so consuming it distorts the perception of reality. Examples from the scriptures show how temptations that seemed so real and enticing at the time involved the enlargement of something trivial that then blocked out the new reality.

Esau must have been genuinely tired and really hungry—nothing imaginary about it—on that occasion when he so desired nourishment that he traded his birthright for a mess of pottage. At this historical distance, however, Esau's transaction, a birthright for a handout, seems incredibly shortsighted; it was not the last time, by the way, that someone gave up so much for a handout.

Thomas B. Marsh's pride, when he supported his wife in a minor dispute concerning cream, ended up causing his excommunication. He had been president of the Council of the Twelve! No doubt, at the time pique piled on pique; but in the perspective of the gospel, what alienated him from his mentor, the Prophet Joseph Smith, was truly trivial. Indeed, until Elder Marsh got past the "milk" stage, there was no gospel "meat" until years later.

Reflect on Cain's quibbling over what to sacrifice, whether or not it was acceptable to the Lord, and the awful deed this led to. His grievances with Abel— imagined or otherwise—no doubt seemed real, but how trivial and then how tragic in the perspective of history! Cain appears to have been not only "a tiller of the ground," but a very careful cultivator of his own ego. Where now are slain Abel's flocks over which Cain gloried when they fell into his hands? (See Moses 5.)

The reasons prompting Lot's wife to take one more tempting look back at Sodom and Gomorrah, instead of being obedient to the command she and Lot had received, were inconsequential in comparison with the consequences of her disobedience. Looking back, said Jesus, will not do for us either. Wistfulness or uncertainty over leaving the ways of the world brought the Master's stern advice to "Remember Lot's wife." (Luke 17:32.)

While our temptations or difficulties are very real, we can pass such breaking points without actually breaking *if we keep our perspective!*

All of this leads to a major point with regard to the challenges of deprivation and tribulation. The immediate and short-run circumstances of the followers of Christ surely differ. Some Church members are divorced. Some are unmarried but long to be married and are worthy to be. Some are widowers, and some are widows. Others are blessed to be in traditional, intact families. Some are healthy; others are ill—some grievously ill. Some are struggling economically; a few are economically quite comfortable. Some are lonely, and others have almost more friends than they can manage. Some are underwhelmed, others overwhelmed with opportunities. Our present circumstances differ sharply, but these will pass away soon enough, though it may seem otherwise at times.

In contrast, our future circumstances and opportunities are strikingly similar. Each of us is a child of God. Each of us agreed to come and pass through this mortal experience. Each of us, if worthy, has the privilege of receiving all the necessary gospel blessings and ordinances. Each of us is loved perfectly by a Heavenly Father who knows us and our needs perfectly. Each of us must walk the same straight and narrow path in order to have happiness here and there. Our fundamental circumstances and opportunities are the same. This should not surprise us, since God is perfectly just.

Now to the major point. A mere hundred years from now today's seeming deprivations and tribulations will not matter *unless we let them matter too much now!* A thousand years from now, for instance, today's serious physical ailment will be but a fleeting memory. A million years from now, those who today worry and are anguished because they are unmarried will, if they are faithful, have smiles of satisfaction on their faces in the midst of a vast convocation of their posterity.

The sense of deprivation that can occur in the life of a single woman in her forties who feels she has no prospects of marriage is real. Yet some deprivations are but delayed blessings, which, if endured well, constitute the readying of reservoirs into which a generous God will pour "all that he hath." Indeed, it will be the Malachi measure: "There shall not be room enough to receive it." (Malachi 3:10.)

In eternity, the insensitivities and injustices of today's grumpy boss will not matter, for we then will live in the presence of a God who is perfect in His justice and His mercy.

A hundred years from now, today's soul pain inflicted by a betraying or deserting spouse will be gone. For those individuals who endure well, all will be well then.

A thousand years from now, if one has been misrepresented or misunderstood, traces of remembrance may remain, but there will be absolutely no resentment.

So it is that in this life, which is such a brief (but very thorough) proving ground, the gospel truths are vital. Do we really believe in these and in ourselves enough to apply them? Are we sufficiently settled to see things as they really are?

If we are true believers, we will be progressing in our discipleship and will thereby maintain our precious perspective.

We will be cheerfully serious about the development of the key eternal attributes and the key everlasting skills in order to increase our capacity to serve others.

We will not resent the fact that this life is a proving ground, because we will understand that our experience here is part of God's purpose for us in the world. Because we come to love and to trust Him, more and more, we can accept even when, at the moment, we do not fully understand His purposes for us and for others.

We will also understand that all of our basic needs are to be met only by keeping His commandments. *There is no other way.*

To see things as they really are *before* that solemn but joyous day when our perspective will be pure is such a blessing. Meanwhile, can we not understand why events that are understandably unwelcome in some ways are, nevertheless, welcome in other ways? A man whose wife lies near death has a precious chance, perhaps for the first time, to put his business —which may have assumed too much size—in proper perspective. It is not a matter of abandoning or devaluing entirely his worthy business but, rather, of putting things in that proportion which comes with being settled—when the objects on the landscape of life assume their true proportion.

If, for instance, next Christmas were to be the last for Grandmother, would we not, without suffocating sentimentality, let some of the Martha-like tasks go undone in order that, Mary-like, Grandmother could be subtly put at the center of things for the last time here?

The Martha-like things chosen are not always the bad part—merely lesser choices. The Savior did not say that the cares of the world were not cares. But this world will pass away, and its cares with it. The things really worth caring about will still be around to be cared about forever. The other things are like last week's firewood, useful to warm a needed meal, which, in turn, helped to sustain the body. But to what end? Only His gospel gives us ultimate reasons. Without such perspective, we would be like astronomers who have never seen the stars.

Thus it is that learning things "according to the flesh" and "in process of time" gives us real and specific opportunities to sort things out, wheat from chaff, as only our individual experience in threshing can do.

Yet another subtle but vital benefit of being grounded, rooted, established, and settled is that time can then work for us. When things are in place, what must happen in process of time can most efficiently occur. When, on the other hand, we are unsettled and drifting as to our beliefs and/or behavior, time is our enemy. Its relentless passage is an unnerving reminder.

When we are not rooted, we feel the heat of the sun quickly and start throwing off that which seems to be disposable in order to be comfortable. Debts are repudiated. Relatives go unacknowledged. Even spouse and children seem to become an extra burden in the heat. The very scorching makes us think, more and more, of our own thirsts and less and less of the discomforts of others, setting in motion an awful cycle within selfishness. Each self-serving step seems to compel another until safety barriers are passed beyond which the victim never really intended to go: "I didn't want to break up my family; I just needed someone to understand me." "We needed the money for the family, and the extra job made sense at the time. Now the reason for the extra money has fallen apart." "The Church calling just didn't fit into my schedule, and now I wonder if the Church can even meet my needs." "There was simply too much tension at home, and the oldest teenagers finally wanted their own apartment. They'll just have to lead their own lives. After all, I'm entitled to a little happiness myself."

So it is that time does not heal all wounds; some wounds widen and worsen.

The cycle of selfishness grimly insures that fewer

and fewer humans will help each other; needs and offerings will match up less and less.

It is not a pretty picture: the lonely crowd, the cacophony in which everybody is asserting and nobody listening, and the demands for *rights* grow, and the pool of those who are willing to assume any *responsibilities* shrinks.

Meanwhile, we will be greatly assisted in our efforts to become *more* grounded, rooted, established, and settled if there is *less* of some things in our lives, such as superficial social settings. With some exceptions, the things that need most to be said and most to be heard occur in one-to-one or small group settings. It is difficult to be profound in a reception line, and time so spent needs to be balanced with time spent in genuine gospel conversation.

To accelerate our becoming more settled spiritually, of what might there be *more?* More time, for instance, to visit the sick, including those in hospitals. Meekly done, it is a help to them and to us, since the blessing of good health is barely noticed when we are "cumbered" with driving on the freeway. Performing the simplest bodily functions and enjoying a good night's sleep are, ironically, taken for granted by us even as God gives them to us day by day. Short stays in and short visits to hospitals can deepen our appreciation. Besides, how many places does one see as much patience as among sensitive doctors, nurses, and orderlies? Or more gratitude than among the sick who, mending, can barely contain their gladness? Hospitals can put things into focus, as can a walk in the woods.

Finally, as we become grounded, rooted, established, and settled, we can stay settled, whether life is unwantedly prolonged or is unexpectedly terminated.

A special young man died some time ago of cancer. David Silvester of Idaho Falls, Idaho, had, for one so young, become grounded, rooted, established, and settled in a very special way. His parents recently shared some excerpts from his journal, words written as he stood on the edge of more life and of a wholly new adventure. These lines illustrate the spiritual maturity so much needed by us all, whether the disciple is needed to go on living or to face dying. David wrote:

Our time should be filled to brimming and then we should ask for more time—and we should love life. . . .

I am not a . . . philosopher—I am a student and my learning shows me new things every day—and God shows me new things every day. I am happy—I pray I will be happy with death.

I enjoy everything about life (almost—sickness and pain aren't too cool) and I still yearn with every particle to be able to marry and have children, and there's so much left to do that I haven't done. . . .

Change. *[Death] is just another change.* Change always gets me nervous and apprehensive and antsy. But I'm always excited by it. Do I have enough time to get my life in order? . . . Maybe I'm . . . an alarmist, but I think the tumor's back . . . and if it is back then it's growing quite rapidly and I probably won't have many months left. One last chance to prove I'm worthy of eternal life with my Heavenly Father. I cried a little (two tears) about it last night.

It is easy to believe in life after death and salvation and exaltation—but to come face to face with it is bewildering. You know . . . that there will be resurrection and assumption of rewards, but what really goes on in "paradise"? How will I receive the pleasure I now do from writing and reading and associating with family and friends? I . . . believe that it will continue there, but I'm still frustrated because I don't want to miss out on everything that is going on here—*but then right now I am missing out on what's going on there.* . . . [Italics added.]

What a marvelous young man, and what a powerful example he and his parents have been! David could not have written that breathtaking passage so serenely unless he had been settled in his faith. The scorching sun of sickness could not dry up David's devotion. A tumor took away his life but not his faith. Having become established spiritually while here, he, no doubt, was quickly established in his new work there, beyond the veil, which, after all, for each of us is just a final heartbeat away.

Chapter Two

"Such As Is Common to Man"

(1 Corinthians 10:13)

In the terse communique from the Gods—"And we will prove them herewith, to see if they will do all things whatsoever the Lord their God shall command them" (Abraham 3:25)—there is a pithy but sweeping declaration of divine intent concerning the mortal experience. This intent has been carried out in terms of how this second estate was to be structured. To misunderstand the message about the purpose of this life as a proving process is to make a fundamental error that insures that thousands of additonal errors will naturally follow.

Surely the Lord, who for the proving of man so carefully created this marvelous "school," this planet —with such incredible interwoven balances in the ecology, the chemistry, and the climate—did not leave unattended the matter of the "curriculum" to be offered.

Furthermore, in a busy, people-filled world, it may seem to us that the school of life contains nothing but large, impersonal classes. Actually, life's lessons are usually learned in a tutorial setting. And our Tutor loves us perfectly, which makes His omniscience a cause for adoration rather than fear.

Isaiah said this earth was formed to be inhabited. (Isaiah 45:18.) Therefore, it can fairly be assumed that at least as much divine attention and forethought were given to the nature of the human experience our Father's children would undergo here as were given to creating this earth. A perfectly just and loving Father, deeply concerned that we learn while here, would provide, among other things, many pervasive, educationally enhancing conditions, such as those that follow:

A deep, deep commitment to human free agency to assure our growth and to make certain that no justified challenge could be made later that our second estate was marred by a lack of freedom to choose—unless we, against divine counsel, choose to bring less opportunity upon ourselves. Given our imperfections, once freedom was insured there would inevitably be mistakes and faulty choices with pain and suffering. Furthermore, many of our prayers could not be answered without violating someone's freedom. In our decisions and actions, our interdependency insured we would be practicing on each other. Even so, we would be "free to choose," but we would be accountable for those choices.

A commonality of certain challenges with varying degrees but no exceptions.

A guarantee that the challenges would not be more than we mortals could bear. We would not be overprogrammed as to temptation, persecution, and tribulation, for these would not be more than we could bear.

A granting of special blessings, but only when earned, since God is a just God who is no respecter of persons.

A sufficient understanding and acquiescence on our part as to what this second estate would consist of so that we could not later say our agreement to come here was "fraudulently induced." There would be a shared realization before-hand that some attributes and skills could be obtained only by experiencing certain things "according to the flesh" and as a result of learning "in process of time."

Adequate guidance from God—scripture, prophets, the Church, a conscience, and the Holy Ghost to make success in a "proving" world feasible for the faithful.

Support from the Lord during the proving process, with Christ our pattern in all things.

A veil of forgetting drawn over our first estate, lest our proving not be complete.

Under such an educationally enhancing plan, there might be selected, divine interventions (the flood, Sodom), but the mortal scene would be permit-ted largely to run its courses with the attendant conse-quences of misused freedom and misbehavior.

Inevitably, under such a plan, the Lord would be charged unfairly by some mortals with being unin-volved or uncaring. Ironically, the individuals mistak-enly making such charges would, if they understood, be quick to complain if their freedoms were taken away. Yet with the exception of certain tutorial trials, most suffering would be the result of human indiffer-ence to God, not God's indifference to humans.

In this risk-filled world, our vulnerability to the things of the world is actually determined by us, and the Lord's final judgment will find us clearly without excuse. We may wish to plead extenuating circum-stances, but we cannot, because it will be shown, to our later satisfaction, that even these circumstances could have been escaped from or endured righteously. We will openly acknowledge "that all his judgments are just." (See Alma 12:14-15.)

Besides, to reject the world is neither to repudiate

its sunsets, its scenery, its worthy music, nor to dis-count those moments when people rise so remarkably to special challenges. Not at all. The world at its best is good. In fact, it is this world at its best that reminds us of the better world that awaits. When this world moves us, however, from the beautiful to the carnal, from appreciation of God to self-worship, or from humility to self-pity—then the world must be rejected.

Odd, is it not, how mortal melancholy is so often expressed but so seldom diagnosed? The sources of human sadness are ignored while the sadness is reported—sometimes with considerable eloquence. Why not, however, face the fact that (to sample but one generation of songs) the sadness in "the days of wine and roses" comes because of alcoholism. The wistful tears shed for a disappearing "Camelot" are caused by the breach of the seventh commandment. The forlornness of lyrics that ask, "What's it all about, Alfie?" come out of a sense of purposelessness, or what Malcolm Muggeridge has called the "over-whelming longing to be in contact with reality."[9] Only the Savior's gospel can tell us about "things as they really are, and . . . really will be." (Jacob 4:13.)

After all, even the melancholy in mortal music be-speaks a sense of happiness that either has been lost or is yearned for. Given who we mortals actually are and what we once knew and experienced, such yearnings should not surprise us in the least.

Without the illumination of the gospel, however, the sense of dread, or angst, will increase. Existential despair will deepen, for *angst* comes from *anomie*, drift and disorientation. There is no genuine succor or so-lace for these symptoms in secularism, because *angst* and *anomie* grow like fungus in a setting that features *anarchy* as to moral values.

Let mortals, if they wish, use their freedom to
mock God; He will not cease loving them, but neither
will He be mocked. Let mortals, if they are so unwise,
curse God and wish to die, but one day they will still
fall into the net of the unearned resurrection. After all,
man is that he *might* have joy—not that he *will* have
joy.

If we understand the scriptures, we should not be
surprised when temptations and trials come to us. We
will also know that the trials of life are meted out to the
faithful (though it seems at times these challenges
come in clusters) in such a way that we are not asked to
endure more than we can bear. The margin of safety
seems thin at times, but it is there.

The mortal experience is, indeed, well structured.
But penalties for wrong-doing are not always immediately extracted. Yes, there is a spiritual ecology the
violation of which brings consequences, but often
without visibility or immediacy.

Walter Bagehot described it superbly:

> *If* the universe were to be incessantly expressive and inces-
> santly communicative, morality would be impossible: we should
> live under the unceasing pressure of a supernatural interference,
> which would give us selfish motives for doing everything, which
> would menace us with supernatural punishment if we left any-
> thing undone; we should be living in a *chastising* machine. . . . The
> life which we lead and were meant to lead would be impossible;
> . . . true virtue would become impossible. . . . A sun that shines
> and a rain which falls equally on the evil and on the good, are es-
> sential to morality in a being free like man and created as man
> was. A miscellaneous world is a suitable theater for a single-
> minded life, and so far as we can see, the only one.[10]

Christians living in the City of Man can attest that it
is so, for we "overcome by faith." (D&C 76:53.) The
scriptures say that the Lord will not give us more than

we can bear if we are humble, since His grace is sufficient for the meek. When our problems, including the particularized thorns in the flesh, seem to contain almost too much trial and tribulation, let us not forget that God has also promised His grace will be sufficient for us. He who structured this school of life with such particularity watches His pupils with exceeding care and knows when we need His grace. He also knows when we need the spur of circumstance.

Paul opened the window of his soul to teach us this basic lesson:

"And lest I should be exalted above measure through the abundance of the revelations, *there was given to me a thorn in the flesh*, the messenger of Satan to buffet me, lest I should be exalted above measure.

"For this thing I besought the Lord thrice, that it might depart from me.

"And he said unto me, *My grace is sufficient for thee*: for my strength is made perfect in weakness." (2 Corinthians 12:7-9. Italics added.)

Moroni both confirmed and amplified this vital doctrine, saying:

"And when I had said this, the Lord spake unto me, saying: Fools mock, but they shall mourn; and *my grace is sufficient for the meek*, that they shall take no advantage of your weakness;

"And if men come unto me I will show unto them their weakness. *I give unto men weakness that they may be humble*; and my grace is sufficient for all men that humble themselves before me; for *if they humble* themselves before me, and have faith in me, then will I make *weak things become strong* unto them." (Ether 12:26-27. Italics added.)

Even so, it is not uncommon for individuals to feel that the temptations and the trials they face are simply too much for them to manage. Happily, we can feel overwhelmed and yet not be overwhelmed, but self-pity adds to our vulnerability. Paul gave us, therefore, a much-needed promise when he wrote this to the saints at Corinth: "There hath no temptation taken you but *such as is common to man*: but God is faithful, who will not suffer you to be tempted above that ye are able; but will with temptation also *make a way to escape*, that *ye may be able to bear it.*" (1 Corinthians 10:13. Italics added.)

Certain temptations are common to those who come to this earth. It is our task to deal with these common temptations in an uncommon manner. The Lord has promised to succor us in our temptations, reminding us that He "knoweth the weakness of man and how to succor them who are tempted." (D&C 62:1.) He truly knows our infirmities firsthand because He has actually borne them. (Alma 7:11-12.)

By succoring us, however, He does not mean He will indulge us. In fact, He will sometimes jar us out of our dreaminess. George MacDonald, a Scottish minister and writer of yesteryear, observed, "It is not the hysterical alone for whom the great dash of cold water is good. All·who dream life instead of living it, require some similar shocks."[11] As Malcolm Muggeridge has observed, "suffering, affliction, disappointment, failure—all these things—are an integral part of the drama of our human existence, and without them there'd be no drama."[12]

Nor should we make the further mistake of thinking that our temptations come from God. James said it very bluntly, almost as if in wearying interviews with Church members he had, by then, heard the same lame excuses too many times:

"Blessed is the man that endureth temptation: for

when he is tried, he shall receive the crown of life, which the Lord hath promised to them that love him.

"Let no man say when he is tempted, I am tempted of God: for *God cannot be tempted* with evil, *neither tempteth he any man:*

"But *every man is tempted,* when he is drawn away *of his own lust,* and enticed." (James 1:12-14. Italics added.)

Lust, that corruption of God-given qualities of pro-creation, is *not* one of the weaknesses or afflictions given to us by God, though it remains for us to over-come.

Peter promised: "The Lord knoweth how to deliver the godly out of temptations." (2 Peter 2:9.) The same promise was reaffirmed in this dispensation: "Verily, thus saith the Lord unto you whom I love, and whom I love I also chasten that their sins may be forgiven, for with the chastisement *I prepare a way for their deliverance* in all things out of temptation." (D&C 95:1. Italics added.)

We are promised deliverance, but the Lord will not kidnap us. The ground rules about free agency insure that we will not be held hostage against our will. Countless times, however, some mortals have insisted on breaking away from His saving grasp in order that they might swim *back* to the sinking ship!

The promise given through Paul that we will not be overwhelmed is echoed in other scriptures (see, for example, D&C 64:20), and it is amplified in the Book of Mormon: "But that ye would humble yourselves be-fore the Lord, and call on his holy name, and *watch and pray* continually, *that ye may not be tempted above that which ye can bear,* and thus be led by the Holy Spirit." (Alma 13:28. Italics added.)

Presumably, to "watch and pray" means having a

realistic regard for the power of temptation and a humble estimation of our own powers to resist it.

In connection with this basic doctrine, the Lord has promised certain things with regard to temptation and tribulation: (1) He has promised to make provisions for us to escape, and these exits *are* there, if we are not so busy looking for ways into, rather than ways out of, temptation. There is always the exit route Joseph courageously used when enticed by Potiphar's wife—he fled. (2) The Lord has also promised to succor us by helping us to bear and to endure. If we could but surrender worthily to Him, once and for all, it would save us so many other unworthy capitulations.

The model with regard to resisting temptation, as in all things, is the Savior Himself. He not only bore tribulations *but also resisted temptations*, far beyond any we can possibly imagine. Paul reminded us of this reality in these verses to the Hebrews:

"For in that he himself hath suffered being tempted, he is able to succour them that are tempted." (Hebrews 2:18.)

"For we have not an high priest which cannot be touched with the feeling of our infirmities; but was in all points tempted like as we are, yet without sin." (Hebrew 4:15.)

Though He was thus perfected in His empathy because He bore our mistakes, Jesus' own response to the common challenges of temptation that faced Him was not only uncommon, it was utterly unique. His immensely important, but simple, key was: "He suffered temptations but *gave no heed unto them*." (D&C 20:22. Italics added.) What a grand yet practical insight! Some of us process the same temptations time and time again, letting them linger and savoring them, and thereby strengthening our impulse to sin and weakening our will to resist—rather than dispatching the temptations summarily as Jesus did when He "gave no heed." Giving no heed includes recognizing for what it is an inducement to do wrong and refusing to consider it further. There is great strength in reflexive rejection and in refusing to spend any of our time, talent, thought, or treasure in hosting a temptation, which is enlarged by any attention given to it.

Unlike Jesus, sometimes we first provide access for and then augment our own temptations. By paying even small heed to a temptation, we thus forget that temptations are like a poison gas—they spread through the time and space available to them. Once inside and unrebuked, they are not easily contained.

Another advantage of dispatching temptations is this: The human mind is remarkably retentive. We must be careful of what we allow in our mind, for it will be there for a long time, reasserting itself at those very times when we may be most vulnerable. Just as harmful chemicals heedlessly dumped in a vacant lot can later prove lethal, so toxic thoughts and the mulching of the wrong memories in the vacant corner of the mind also take their toll.

What happens, of course, when we persist in savoring temptations, whether they are temptations of wealth, power, status, or sensuality, is well portrayed by what we read of another people in another time: "Now the cause of this iniquity of the people was this—Satan had great power, unto the stirring up of the people to do all manner of iniquity, and to the puffing them up with pride, *tempting them to seek for power, and authority, and riches*, and the vain things of the world." (3 Nephi 6:15. Italics added.)

This people actually lost both personal *and* social control, as these words vividly portray: "And thus, in the commencement of the thirtieth year—the people having been delivered up for the space of a long time to be *carried about by the temptations of the devil whithersoever he desired to carry them,* and to do whatsoever iniquity he desired they should—and thus in the commencement of this, the thirtieth year, they were in a state of awful wickedness." (3 Nephi 6:17. Italics added.)

Surely it should give us more pause than it does to think of how casually we sometimes give to him who could not control his own ego in the premortal world such awful control over our egos here. We often let the adversary do *indirectly* now what we refused to let him do *directly* then.

Thus we can expect no immunity from either trial or temptation, because these are the common lot of mankind. Mortality without the dimension of temptation or trial would not be a full proving; it would be a school with soft credits and no hard courses. These features of mortality were among the very conditions we agreed to before we undertook this mortal experience. We cannot renege on that commitment now. We are encountering not only divine love but also divine determination concerning this plan of happiness, for "there is nothing that . . . God shall take into his heart to do but what he will do it." (Abraham 3:17.)

So it is that the real but unheralded heroes and heroines of our time are the men and women of the earth who uncommonly resist the world's common temptations, who surmount the common tribulations of the world and continue to the very end in righteousness, arriving home battered slightly, yet much bettered. Such individuals may get little mortal applause or recognition, but there is real rejoicing elsewhere by those who really know what a good performance is!

Chapter Three

"According to the Flesh" and "In Process of Time"

(Alma 7:11-12; Moses 7:21)

Two seldom-cited scriptural concepts can help us understand and accept the realities of this proving life with the temptations and challenges that are common to man. These verses provide a perspective about mortality that is truly essential.

Jesus, who is our advocate with the Father, knows "the weakness of man," and He also knows "how to succor them who are tempted." (D&C 62:1.) How does He know? Does He know by inference or only in the abstract? A special scripture tells us. He knows by actual, personal experience, because not only did He suffer pains, afflictions, and temptations of every kind during His second estate, but He took upon Himself our sins as well as our pains, sicknesses, and infirmities. (See Alma 7:11-12.) Thus He knew, not in abstraction but in actuality, "according to the flesh," the whole of human suffering. He bore our infirmities before we bore them. He knows perfectly well how to succor us. We can tell Him nothing of pain, temptation, or affliction; He learned "according to the flesh," and His triumph was complete!

46

We, too, must learn "according to the flesh." There is no other way. A second scripture is relevant. In this proving process, the seasoning of would-be saints occurs not in a day but "in process of time" as it did in the refining of those in the City of Enoch. (See Moses 7:21, 68-69.) The virtues and qualities to be acquired do not spring forth in a day or even a decade.

As we face the frustrations and challenges as well as the joys of living, we are helped in becoming grounded, rooted, established, and settled if we note that this mortal experience is planned so that we learn those things which can only be learned "according to the flesh." (Alma 7:11-12.) How else could we really learn patience, a virtue that simply can't be acquired in the abstract? How could we ever learn to forgive till we have been stung and realize the need to forgive the individual who has stung us? Or, even more poignantly, until we have wronged someone and deeply desire his forgiveness? Clearly, whatever degree of spiritual progress we achieved in the first estate, certain experiences are unique with the second estate. Some of the curriculum carries over, but certain "courses" are offered for the first time here in mortality. Such experiences are largely those associated with learning to subject a mortal body to the things of the Spirit, such as in connection with the law of chastity.

In the tender and even scriptural letter sent by the Prophet Joseph Smith to a repentant W. W. Phelps, who had betrayed the Prophet, there is this great generosity and eloquence. Without this redemptive reach of Joseph's, as Elder Boyd K. Packer has pointed out, would we now be singing Brother Phelps' "Gently Raise the Sacred Strain," "Come, All Ye Sons of God," "The Spirit of God Like a Fire," and "Praise to the Man"?

DEAR BROTHER PHELPS:—I must say that it is with no ordinary feelings I endeavor to write a few lines to you . . . at the same time I am rejoiced at the privilege granted me.

You may in some measure realize what my feelings . . . were, when we read your letter—truly our hearts were melted into tenderness and compassion when we ascertained your resolves, &c. I can assure you I feel a disposition to act on your case in a manner that will meet the approbation of Jehovah, (whose servant I am), and agreeable to the principles of truth and righteousness which have been revealed; and inasmuch as long-suffering, patience, and mercy have ever characterized the dealings of our heavenly Father towards the humble and penitent, I feel disposed to copy the example, cherish the same principles, and by so doing be a savior of my fellow men.

It is true, that we have suffered much in consequence of your behavior—the cup of gall, already full enough for mortals to drink, was indeed filled to overflowing when you turned against us. One with whom we had oft taken sweet counsel together, and enjoyed many refreshing seasons from the Lord—"had it been an enemy, we could have borne it." . . .

However, the cup has been drunk, the will of our Father has been done, and we are yet alive, for which we thank the Lord. And having been delivered from the hands of wicked men by the mercy of our God, we say it is your privilege to be delivered from the powers of the adversary, be brought into the liberty of God's dear children, and again take your stand among the Saints of the Most High, and by diligence, humility, and love unfeigned, commend yourself to our God, and your God, and to the Church of Jesus Christ.

Believing your confession to be real, and your repentance genuine, I shall be happy once again to give you the right hand of fellowship, and rejoice over the returning prodigal.

Your letter was read to the Saints last Sunday, and an expression of their feeling was taken, when it was unanimously *Resolved*, That W. W. Phelps should be received into fellowship.

"Come on, dear brother, since the war is past,
For friends at first, are friends again at last."
Yours as ever,
JOSEPH SMITH, JUN.[13]

Could the Prophet Joseph Smith have written such

a letter ten years earlier when he was less spiritually mature? Or really learned to forgive the repentant betrayer *in the abstract* without the actual experience? Could the Great Physician train us fully without our painfully practicing on each other, since we are each other's clinical material in mortality?

So it is that there are some things to be learned "according to the flesh." Temptation could not be genuinely overcome if experienced only in the abstract. Nor could persecution be coped with by proxy.

Likewise, there are some things to be accomplished only "in process of time." Therefore, such proving and learning can be accomplished only by our mortal experience, and even this occurs not suddenly, but "in process of time." Can we be truly trained without this rigorous "residency" on this planet? Thus when the phrase "in process of time" is used in the scriptures, it does not always merely mean "eventually," but connotes a process.

Given this recurring reality—against which we should not kick—there should be no mystery about why life must be as it is. If we can but accept the realities that emerge from these two teachings, things would be seen more simply and more accurately. There would be less murmuring and less going against the gospel grain.

We could better understand when the encrustations of ego are sometimes broken off suddenly by events, but also how it is that the abruptness and the bleeding often merely result in their regrowth. More often, preparatory softening "in process of time" causes the ripe crust of ego to fall off almost as a part of the healing.

But there is still more to flow from the juxtaposition

of these two doctrines. Sometimes the very individuals who are meeting life's challenges reasonably well still fail to appreciate the adequacy and efficacy of their response. They are coping and growing but sometimes without the quiet, inner-soul satisfaction that can confirm genuine progress.

The lingering sense that certain individuals have that there is something more they should be doing detracts, quite needlessly, from the inward satisfaction that could offset their weariness. A few who are reasonably diligent still seem badgered by the feeling that there is a lack of full significance in their lives. The chores being done are viewed by them as, somehow, not quite what was really expected of them. There is divine purpose, therefore, in the Lord's encouraging us not to weary of well-doing in the seemingly ordinary life. We are to trust in the purposefulness of life even when life seems commonplace.

True, there are more things to be done than we do, more opportunities for service than are used. True, we make mistakes, and even some of our achievements are flawed by our lack of finesse. True, there are flat periods in life when we may feel underwhelmed. But if there is any surprise about this second estate and the lessons to be learned "according to the flesh," and if there is any central truth to be grasped regarding personal development "in process of time," it is this: there is no hidden purpose!

There are no chores of reforming exterior institutions that diminish the basic challenge of self reform. There is no new, stunning truth about the process of life that will cause us to gasp in surprise. The communiqué about divine intent to prove us is the *summum bonum.* (Abraham 3:25.)

But it is enough!

Therefore, those who expect some sudden, sweeping insight about this life—heretofore inscrutably withheld from us—may find the truth about this life as a proving place quite pedestrian. The criterion, however, for assessing the gospel has never been "Is it exotic?," but rather, "Is it true?" Our surprises are far more likely to occur when some plain truth that we have known all along is suddenly or dramatically confirmed anew.

Those who would like more mystique about mortality should be grateful for the plainness and the simplicity of the way. Otherwise, we too might be given over (in our desire for complexity) to things that we cannot understand and thereby end up "looking beyond the mark." (Jacob 4:14.)

Furthermore, the process of becoming settled in our faith and established in our righteousness— imperfect as we are—obviously does not suggest a sporadic attachment to values nor a nomadic approach to finding our way; one does not, later on, leave the straight and narrow path to pursue the road "not taken."

There will be adventures enough in becoming settled. Sweet, private spiritual experiences will occur. Added gifts of the Spirit will be given "for the benefit of those who love me and keep all my commandments," or who "seeketh so to do." (D&C 46:9.) Thus, while our individual agendum of life is filled with that which is common to man, our experiences can be uncommon, too. Having kept our first estate by being faithful in the premortal world, we are ready now to "be added upon." But the added weight can best be sustained if we are fully grounded.

Once settled in "holy places," the task for the disciple is to "stand . . . and . . . not be moved." (D&C

45:32.) Those who waver in their steadfastness for fear they are missing out will miss out. Those who fret lest the seeming mundaneness of their mortal passage implies that they thereby are shortchanged would do well to recall what those were told who inquired of the Lord as to what they could do of "most worth" to help His work along. They were told, quite simply, to get their lives in order and to declare repentance unto this generation. No mention was made of improving Congress or a nation's monetary policy, important as these may be for the moment.

Those who desire sweeping significance and high visibility in the second estate should confront themselves honestly with certain questions.

Is it numbers of people touched *at that moment* that measures the impact of an individual? Did tens of thousands hear the Sermon on the Mount? Did it make the six o'clock news? How many stayed with Him through Calvary?

Was Abraham to have been measured by the volume of his trade with nomads in the desert? Or by his living so as to see, one day, the promise fulfilled that his posterity would be as numberless as the stars in the heavens? (Genesis 22:17.) Was Ruth's eloquent and touching entreaty to Naomi to be measured for its significance by the size of her audience?

Or is it the terrain one traverses that is the true test of his life? If so, how shall those of us who travel in the jet age assess the mileage logged by Jesus during His mortal ministry? In those days, from Dan to Beersheba seemed so sweeping, yet it involved only a little over a hundred miles. One day, our sweeping travels about this globe today will seem to us quite provincial when we are wafted from planet to planet.

President Brigham Young in 1866 sent the first

message over the Deseret Telegraph, a marvel in its time, but even then he saw more distantly: "I dedicate the line which is now completed to the Lord God of Israel whom we serve and for the building up of His Kingdom praying that this and all other improvements may contribute to our benefit and the glory of God until we can waft ourselves by the power of the Almighty from worlds to worlds to our fullest satisfaction."

But in a day when empires fall and terrorists hold nations hostage, does focusing on one's little family or neighborhood seem too tiny a concern? In any event, if being startled is what we desire, let us save some room for wonder as the moment arrives when the eternal family's ultimate itinerary is fully unveiled!

Even so, some may still say, "I know I am not doing all I could, so how could what I am doing be enough?" Ah, but that is *not* the real question. The real question is, "Why should I desire more than to perform the work to which I have been called?" (Alma 29:6.) That is the question—for a mother, son, home teacher, Young Woman's leader, elders quorum president, or neighbor. The task is, therefore, to perform in one's callings. On that score each of us should seek to do more. But it is not another task we should seek!

Of the sobering but mist-dispelling truths— "according to the flesh" and "in process of time"—it must be said, finally, there is no other way. (Alma 38:9.) And even these five words should be spoken reverently—not in disappointed resignation, but with an attitude of gratefulness. If we sigh a bit, it should be a reassuring sigh that spurs us to shoulder our packs again and to move on, carrying only the essentials, for once we know in the center of our souls that there is no other way, there will be, instead of oppressive weariness, resilience that is born of reassurance. Why look back for long when so much lies ahead?

Such basic gospel truths put not only the purpose of life in bold perspective, but also human events. We have a frame of reference within which to view other things. We can understand what is truly and everlastingly important as contrasted with what we mortals sometimes exclaim over in our understandable but childish enthusiasms of the moment. Without such truth-trained perspective, we may become like economist and free trader, Richard Cobden, who said in 1846 that the repeal of England's Corn Laws was "the most important event in history since the coming of Christ." As important as that legislation may have been, clearly Cobden was carried away, and not by the Spirit!

President Richard Nixon in 1969 described two American men's walking on the moon as being part of "the greatest week in the history of the world since the creation." Though his pride and enthusiasm were understandable, the exaggeration took no note of the Atonement or the Resurrection.

Edward Norman made these observations about the Christian and his relationship to changing human campaigns and enthusiasms: "At the centre of the Christian religion, Christ remains unchanging in a world of perpetual social change and mutating values. To identify him with the passing enthusiasms of men—each one of which, in its time of acceptance, seems permanently true—is to lose him amidst the shifting superstructure of human idealism."[14]

Let us, armed with such perspective, remember that the great redeeming plan of salvation of God over which, in the premortal world, we once shouted for joy was clearly worth shouting over; mere human events are something else. Civilizations and institutions may tumble, for there is only one thing against which "the gates of hell" will not prevail—God's work!

After finding and accepting God and putting things in proper perspective, we should then also understand that, within the larger plan of salvation, with its commonality in certain of our challenges there are also complementary, individual plans for all of us, and each is enfolded into God's overall plan. Therefore, let us believe and trust in God enough that He can see us through our common challenges and on to the finish of our plans. If we will but humbly trust Him and have faith in Him, then His grace will be sufficient for us. (2 Corinthians 12:7-9; Ether 12:26-27.)

Great rewards come to us when we respond to common challenges uncommonly. By living righteously, being settled, established, grounded, and rooted in the Savior, we have adventure-filled experiences that those who only "for a while believe" never do have.

Given the perfect justice of God, who is no respecter of persons, the commonness of certain challenges should not surprise us. We could complain if God were not just; but given the reality that all will not only finally acknowledge on bended knee (with some assuming that posture for that purpose for the first time) and with confessing tongue that Jesus is the Christ (with some forming those words, except in profanity, for the first time), is it not, therefore, understandable that the human drama must play itself out as an everlasting record, clear and unmistakable?

Since there is no other way for human happiness than God's way, will it not need to be abundantly evident that man's ways simply do not work in the common experience of the shared second estate? In order for all to accept the judgments preceding immortality (*without* being able to assert either that we were not "free to choose" or that our substitute schemes had no chance to be proven demonstrably inadequate), could it be otherwise than as arranged? Is not the promised universal acknowledgment of God's justice and His mercy a feeling that must last, so that there can be absolutely no hedging, even inwardly, thereafter? And no equivocation, subsequently, to qualify our full confessions of His Lordship?

The record, individual and collective, will be so undeniable and so unarguably clear that none—not one—can dispute the fact that a loving Father left us free to choose, that He "forced no man to heaven," that the wisdom of man proved to be comparative foolishness, and that when men, instead of walking in the straight and narrow path, walked in their own way—misery and tragedy occurred, again and again!

Just how God will ensure such a replay of human history we do not know fully, but as Brother Roy W. Doxey has written: "The Lord has revealed that for each of the seven thousand years of earth's temporal existence since Adam's fall, men's acts have been recorded. The revealing of the secret acts of men and 'the thoughts and intents of their hearts' and the mighty works of God in each one of these seven periods, will occur during the millennial period of peace and brotherhood upon the earth. (D&C 88:108-110; 77:6-7, 12.)"[15]

We do know, individually, that we shall have a bright recollection of our guilt and a perfect remembrance of our past. (Alma 5:18; 11:43.) If needed, there could be a collective equivalent in which human folly is graphically recounted, so that all will be forever disabused of any mistaken, provincial, or lingering notions about what really happened during the second estate.

Very importantly, we know that our memories of the first estate will eventually be fully restored; and, upon regaining our premortal perspectives, we will acknowledge that we did indeed come here under certain conditions to which we earlier agreed—with the risks and rewards adequately explained beforehand.

Only with such a final cleansing of our perceptions about mortality could we then, profitably and without disabling backward glances, get on with immortality and eternal life. Perhaps this is part of what it means when a prophet said, "They that murmured shall learn doctrine." (Isaiah 29:24.)

Moreover, with one group's exception, each of us will go to a kingdom of glory. (D&C 88:24.) Knowing as we do the beauties of this earth, which the Lord described as "good," can we not quiver just a bit in anticipation of those kingdoms that He calls not only good, but also places of "glory"? God is not given to hyperbole!

Thus we shall be filled with everlasting gratitude for that which God in His mercy provides in each of the degrees of glory. We shall not question His justice, for He is perfect in His attribute of justice. Of course, in each of our cases we will perceive what might have been, but even so, we can only be content with our allotment given our "on-the-record" performance on this planet combined with the carryover from our first estate. We will have had our chance "according to the flesh" and "in process of time."

In the sobering events that are impending in the playing-out of human history, we can better understand why this must be so. Even the martyrdom of certain saints has been permitted so that the record can be clear. (D&C 88:94.) If the judgments of God were to come upon mankind *in advance* of wickedness, then God would not be a just God.

Hence, when we mortals groan under the circumstances of sin—global or individual—this too is part of experiencing things "according to the flesh." Are there no divine interventions under special circumstances? Yes, such as in the Noachian flood and in the cases of Sodom and Gomorrah, when corruption had reached an agency-destroying point that spirits could not, in justice, be sent here. President John Taylor said: "Because in forsaking God, they lose sight of their eternal existence, corrupt themselves, and entail misery on their posterity. Hence it was better to destroy a few individuals, than to entail misery on many. And hence the inhabitants of the old world and of the cities of Sodom and Gomorrah were destroyed, because it was better for them to die, and thus be deprived of their agency, which they abused, than entail so much misery on their posterity, and bring ruin upon millions of unborn persons."[16]

Then, too, just prior to the very end the Lord has said He will shorten the days before His coming for the sake of the elect. (Matthew 24:22.) God's mercy and love interact with His justice, so that what is needed, according to His omniscience, is done. Later, we shall see fully that what was done was wise and just.

Meanwhile, as things so painfully play themselves out, we would do well to remind ourselves that it will be thus, and that God's commitment to our agency is, fortunately, much deeper and consistent than our own. Mortals will be left without excuse, atheists and disciples alike.

Unless mankind repents, however, as in the case of ancient Ninevah, the prophesied events will occur.

This means that a "desolating sickness," not just some isolated cases of the flu, "shall cover the land"; "the love of men shall wax cold," not just indifference and insensitivity to others; and "iniquity shall abound," not just an upsurge in shoplifting. Even in the midst of such desolations "men will harden their hearts against me." (D&C 45:31, 27, 33.)

As we "shall see all these things" in that summer, we shall "know that the hour is nigh." (D&C 45:38.) Since these are not trivial events, they will get our firsthand attention. Of the fig trees in that special summer the Lord reminded us, "Ye see them with your eyes." (D&C 45:37.) The signs will be unmistakable but must be viewed in their totality lest one sign be mistaken for them all. Peace has been taken from the earth, as the First Presidency observed in 1852:

Since our last Epistle, of October 3, 1852, we know of but few particulars that have transpired among the various nations of the earth. But we know that the revelations of Jesus Christ are true, and that peace is taken from the earth, and that those who will not receive and obey the Gospel of Jesus Christ, when they hear it, will grow worse and worse, in evil passions, strife, war, and blood, until the wicked shall have overthrown the wicked and destroyed themselves from the face of the earth (Sec. 63:32-33; 87:6), that Jesus may have the privilege to reign unmolested in the midst of those that love him. (MS 15:437, July 9, 1853.)[17]

We will thus experience, "according to the flesh," consequences of that lamentable but foreseen condition (D&C 1:35) when war will be almost a continuum. The Lord has promised that during the travail preceding His coming He will be in the midst of His saints and will reign and watch over them. (D&C 1:36.) This is prior to the majestic circumstance, however, when He comes in triumph and visible power to reign over all the earth.

Being in the midst of His saints involves the directing of His Church and giving unto faithful members sufficient grace to see them through tribulation. He can be in our midst, exerting His influence and bringing to pass His purposes, without our seeing Him. (D&C 38:7; 49:27.) Those who have oil in their lamps will know assuredly of the directing presence of the Bridegroom!

This sobering but grand reality is but another example of why it is wise, at least sometimes, to think of faith in the Lord in terms of trust, *deep trust*. It is also an example of how essential it is for us "in process of time" to be patient in affliction, ever avoiding the temptation, as the judgments of God come upon mankind and we experience things "according to the flesh," to charge God foolishly. (Job 1:22.) There will be enough others doing that! (Mormon 2:14; D&C 45:32.)

Chapter Four

Everlasting Skills and Eternal Attributes

In view of why we are here on this planet, more than occasional consideration should be given to the outcomes we are striving to achieve. Indeed, we would do well to ponder more often than we do just what it is that "will rise with us in the resurrection." (D&C 130:18-19.)

We are to develop certain eternal attributes and to acquire certain everlasting skills. These attributes and skills are never obsolete. They are portable, being essential not only in this, our second estate, but in our third and everlasting estate.

Though numerous scriptures speak of these qualities to be developed, there is a recurring cluster of adjectives to describe the eternal attributes. In Mosiah, we read that a saint is one who is *meek, humble, patient, full of love,* and who is sufficiently *submissive* that he can cope with "all things which the Lord seeth fit to inflict upon him even as a child doth submit to his father." (Mosiah 3:19.) Parallel insights occur in Alma, who stressed our need to become *humble, submissive, gentle, easy to be entreated,* and *patient.* (Alma 7:23.)

Elsewhere, the message is the same, whether it is Micah (6:8) speaking of the importance of *justice, mercy,* and *humility* or *meekness,* or the Prophet Joseph Smith's declarations concerning how the grand attributes of God, who is *perfect* in such qualities as *love* and *mercy,* should be firmly linked to Jesus' call for us to become perfect even as our Father in heaven is perfect! (Matthew 4:48.) Being perfect is not a vague, generalized condition, but the acquiring of key attributes. Our Father is described not only as omnipotent and omniscient, but also as having ultimate capacity in *justice* and *mercy.*

These qualities, therefore, are those we are either to acquire or to develop much more deeply. C. S. Lewis observed that we must realize that God "wants a people of a particular sort," not just obedience to a set of rules.

For perspective, it is interesting to read these words of the Savior about an earlier failure resulting from a lack of perspective and proportion: "Woe unto you, scribes and Pharisees, hypocrites! for ye pay tithe of mint and anise and cummin, and have omitted the *weightier matters* of the law, *judgment, mercy,* and *faith*: these ought ye to have done, and not to leave the other undone." (Matthew 23:23. Italics added.)

Clearly, as the Lord noted, we are still to pay tithing, for it is the Lord's law, and we are not to leave other important things undone. But the *weightier* considerations consist of such qualities as *judgment* or *justice* and *mercy* and *faith.*

The Ten Commandments, carefully scrutinized, can be seen to conform to the two great commandments:

"Master, which is the great commandment in the law?

"Jesus said unto him, Thou shalt love the Lord thy God with all thy heart, and with all thy soul, and with all thy mind.

"This is the first and great commandment.

"And the second is like unto it, Thou shalt love thy neighbour as thyself." (Matthew 22:36-39.)

Each of the eight remaining commandments, in one way or another, bears upon demonstrating our love of God or of our neighbor.

Time and time again, we are exhorted in the scriptures concerning the eternal qualities. Indeed, if we are to serve God well, it requires qualities such as love, knowledge, patience, and humility. (D&C 4:5-6.) The glorious Beatitudes also draw our attention to meekness, humility, mercy, and peacemaking. (Matthew 5:3-11; Luke 6:20-22.)

Nephi advises us that our very capacity to stay on the straight and narrow path would require developing to a significant degree our capacity to love God and all men. We would also be helped along the way if we would "feast," as Nephi said, on the word of Christ and then endure to the end. (2 Nephi 31:20.)

The development of these attributes gives evidence that we are becoming settled in our allegiance to God. Otherwise, our ambivalence shows itself again and again.

Does not our tendency to give alms before men suggest that we prefer their praise to His?

Does not our concern over our seemingly unnoticed virtue mean either that we doubt His omniscience or that pleasing Him does not yet mean enough?

Does not our complaint that others are not doing their part—even if justified—imply that our partnership with the Lord in serving others is a limited partnership, except, of course, when we need blessings from Him?

Does not our feeling that certain forms of Christian service are a bother let us know how much like the busy Levite who passed on the other side we sometimes are?

Does not our occasional unwillingness to forget another's past suggest our desire, though undeclared, to keep him in his place? We let the prodigal have his welcome-home feast, but do not let the evening end without mentioning his past harlotry.

So vital is this perspective about the outcomes to be achieved in the school of life, in experiences to be felt "according to the flesh" and "in process of time," that it must not be lost amid the shuffling of trivia.

Perspective is precious and is especially needed when differing claims compete for our time and talents, as this secular illustration conveys: "In 1918 Ernest Rutherford, a physicist, missed a meeting of experts advising the British government on anti-submarine warfare. When criticized, he replied: 'I have been engaged in experiments which suggest that the atom can be artificially disintegrated. If it is true, it is of far greater importance than a war.' "[18]

Our purposes on this planet must not be obscured by wars and rumors of wars. Just as the splitting of the atom was of far more significance than a mere meeting on anti-submarine warfare, so the development of the eternal attributes is far more important than the usual focal points of the busyness of our lives.

Even in our Church chores the need for these desired attributes must be kept before us. Otherwise, as has been said, we can be consumed by our busyness rather than pursuing our fundamental purposes. Without clearly defined goals, most mortals concentrate on activity with the real risk of becoming enslaved by it.

It should not surprise us that we need to be schooled in lesser laws on our way to acquiring the eternal attributes. For instance, as we strive for love or humility in relationship to our fellowmen, we can commence by practicing the schoolmaster virtue of politeness. Of politeness G. K. Chesterton wisely said: "Politeness is not really a frippery. Politeness is not really even a thing merely suave and deprecating. Politeness is an armed guard, stern and splendid and vigilant, watching over all the ways of men; in other words, politeness is a policeman."[19]

But someday the policeman will not be needed, for our love, when more developed, will make courtesy a natural matter of reflex, not a duty or protocol.

These overarchingly important attributes and virtues obviously can be acquired only by the experiences we have "according to the flesh" and "in process of time." They cannot be acquired in the abstract. Programs and activities in the Church as well as the well-used routine of life can do so much to advance us in the acquisition of attributes such as mercy and patience. But we must never lose sight of that toward which we are striving, imprecise and slow as our efforts may seem at times.

Quite understandably, therefore, the Church seeks to avoid the mistakes of some secular governments that establish a program for every need and a department for every constituency. What is needed is more good neighbors and fewer programs. And Church programs and activities should ever facilitate the development of the eternal attributes and skills. Developing humility, love, and meekness, for instance, will be the unconscious result of a consciously chosen way of life, the accumulation of righteous actions in the midst of seeming routine that can hasten the acquisition of these attributes.

Though not cited, *per se*, in the scriptures, it is quite clear that certain skills accompany the eternal attributes, such as love and gentleness, which skills will be everlastingly useful. They too are vital here and will not be obsolete in the world to come. It apparently was necessary to teach Moses, who had already developed his meekness—indeed, who was the meekest man upon the face of the earth (Numbers 12:3)—how to *delegate*. (See Exodus 18.) Surely the promised assignments in the celestial world to come will require us to delegate. Surely our Father in heaven has done that perfectly, inasmuch as He has chosen to share the work in His business with us fumbling mortals.

Likewise, it appears that increasing our capacity to *communicate* as well as to delegate will be everlastingly relevant. Surely our capacity to *motivate* others will be continuously important. So will our capacity to *listen*. One who is grounded, rooted, established, and settled will reflect a listening style, for doing what is right is greatly aided by doing it in the right way. Furthermore, our skills are rooted in and are outward expressions of our attributes.

Superb listening involves patience, meekness, and humility. Real *communicating* is greatly aided by love. *Delegating* would soon be abandoned without loving patience in behalf of those to whom work is given.

Just as the Lord was able to summarize His priorities so succinctly that it is his "work and . . . glory to bring to pass the immortality and eternal life of man" (Moses 1:39), so we, too, will need to be able to manage our time and talents in such a way that we, too, know our real priorities and focus on them. When we are settled in our hearts on that which really matters, then our talent and time as well as our treasure will be thus deployed!

The interlocking of the eternal attributes and everlasting skills is obvious. The risk is that, in the busyness of it all, we will lose sight of these key objectives. We should not be surprised when, though one's capacity to manage self has been demonstrated to mortal satisfaction, the Lord still puts him through a humbling exercise. After all, did not David's later failure occur in the realm of self-management rather than in the management of a kingdom?

The Lord's tutorials make extensive use of props and scenery in this mortal school, but we should not become too fascinated with the schoolhouse or schoolyard to the neglect of the curriculum and the homework required. The Headmaster is not keen either about our "dropping" certain courses just because these have proved difficult.

We must be very careful, therefore, about focusing too much on a technique like waving one's arms and pacing the floor to pressure a group of salesmen, which technique may have no place in the next estate, while, at the same time, we neglect developing the eternal attributes such as love and humility, which will never be obsolete. Nor will a penchant for jargon as a means of demonstrating one's verbal exclusivity be acceptable in the world to come where the test of conversation will be truth and simplicity, spoken in love.

One can, of course, while in the employ of a railroad company, learn something of patience while struggling to keep the schedule up-to-date, but the self-discipline achieved will outlast the usefulness of the schedule. A serious scientist may augment the awe he has for the breathtaking order in the universe and thereby increase his meekness and humility before his Creator—even if the new "laws" just discovered are, ere long, swallowed up in even more immense laws and discoveries.

It is also true that a grave digger may become indifferent not only to the sorrows of the bereaved gathered about the fresh mounds of earth he creates, but also to the resurrection that will one day empty all those carefully dug graves. Likewise, a marriage counselor can become unintentionally encrusted with a protective layer of clinical indifference brought on by the incessant nature of his chores. Techniques bereft of love for his clients will be of little help.

It is left to us in our varied situations to make the interplay of our time and talent and treasure add up to significant accomplishment in our development of the key eternal attributes and the everlasting skills. A botched performance here means fewer skills to serve with there! Any resulting advantage we have in the world to come will result from the added knowledge and the intelligence to apply truth that is acquired here. This advantage will bring added opportunities to serve everlastingly.

Those who are grounded, rooted, established, and settled will take more serious account of the above eternal objectives on which this life should focus than will those who may, for instance, be doing well financially but only as communicators in behalf of some passing product. In like manner, a civil servant who has forgotten how to be civil may have some sway now in the procurement division of a vast governmental department, but he is headed in just the opposite direction needed for sway in the next world. Whatever sharp bargains he strikes in purchases here, he is procuring problems for himself there.

Therefore, in view of how vital these attributes are, one should take exceeding care that his mortal activities do not take him in the opposite developmental direction. Desensitizing circumstances will not aid one in fostering the attribute of mercy. Cutthroat competition will make the second commandment seem an increasingly remote requirement. Being paid for brusqueness will not help one to be easily entreated.

It is true that one can be in a role that is conducive to officiousness and yet be meek therein. Even so, one does not strive to develop film in the plaza at high noon or throw firecrackers about a gasoline station. Life is risk-filled enough without our adding needlessly thereto.

On the other hand, one who listens more and more attentively to others with a genuine desire to understand, if not always to agree, will have no regrets later on. Such an individual may occasionally run out of time and may even be seen by some as needing to be more directive. But what is building can reflect a growing love and patience, and such investments are never wasted—they only appear to be.

The devoted wife and mother who was an effective neighbor but whose obituary is noticed by a comparative few may well have laid up precious little here in the coin of the realm, recognition. Yet rising with her in the resurrection will be the relevant skills, honed and refined in family and neighborhood life. Contrariwise, the civic leader whose thirst for recognition caused what little generosity he displayed here will rate a large obituary, but he has had his recognition and reward—along with the unearned gift of immortality during which he can work on meekness.

Those who pursue sensual pleasures with such intensity lest they miss the last gasp are wrong in what they do, but, ironically, are correct in their acknowledgment that the "streetcar named Desire" does reach the end of its line.

And how many of us spend time in life's midyears in order to accumulate money with which we then turn around in later years and vainly try to buy time? How many striving fathers are so busy getting established economically—a worthy goal—that they have little time now for the children, but hope soon to be in a position to spend more time with the children who, even sooner, are grown or gone?

The eternal attributes yield so many secondary blessings. Sarcasm is nurtured by neither love nor patience. Spouses, for instance, will think of more clever things to say than should be said. Since the "guilty taketh the truth to be hard, for it cutteth them to the very center," all the more reason for us to administer reproof only when moved upon by the Holy Ghost. (1 Nephi 16:2; D&C 121:43.) True love will help us to be just as concerned with *how* we give counsel as with the correctness of the counsel.

The everlasting skills have so much to do with matching our style with the substance of the gospel. Truth makes its way best when accompanied by real love. Even caring candor requires meekness on the part of the receiver. Flippant frankness and insights insensitively given are apt to benefit only the most secure and noble of recipients.

Being full of love for others does not permit rejoicing when trials come to others who have seemed to be free of trials ("It's about their turn"). If it is their "turn," that is a matter between God and them. For our part, there should be prayers, empathy, and even reverence, for souls are clearly at risk.

Among the reasons for not comparing crosses is

the fact that, first, we know so little about the weight of crosses and, second, we know even less about the bearing capacity of their owners. Someone who stumbles with seemingly little weight in one thing may have superb capacity for shouldering certain larger tasks. But the Lord insists on symmetry of soul, so it is not always the dunces who stay "after school." And whenever we think ourselves to be "above all that," we should recall that we are being tutored by Him who "descended below them all." (D&C 122:8.)

One dimension of enduring to the end, by the way, is to maintain the perspective about the proving role of life on this planet. Even the eternal attributes can be lost by foolishness, especially the gradual variety in which what has been slips away, bit by bit.

Take David's purity and humility. These attributes probably exited together. Ponder the sweet boldness of the unspoiled David, who went up against Goliath: "Then said David to the Philistine, Thou comest to me with a sword, and with a spear, and with a shield: but I come to thee in the name of the Lord of hosts, the God of the armies of Israel, whom thou hast defied." (1 Samuel 17:45.)

Then compare this young David with the later, effete David, who indulged himself as only a king can. Courtiers seldom remonstrate with a king, and when his conscience is dulled, the Uriahs of the world are seen as impediments. Indeed, the nobility of soul that once shone about David was now to be found in the loyal but betrayed Uriah, who declined a comfortable resting place: "And Uriah said unto David, The ark, and Israel, and Judah, abide in tents; and my lord Joab, and the servants of my lord, are encamped in the open fields; shall I then go into mine house, to eat and to drink, and to lie with my wife? as thou livest, and as thy soul liveth, I will not do this thing." (2 Samuel 11:11.)

The balances to be struck are not easily achieved, but they are much more often struck if one can react humbly when brought up short in reminder of the real purposes of life.

Often, what seems to be an unwelcome and untimely insertion into our lives may, in fact, be a last chance to regain the precious perspective of the gospel and to further refine a trait that transcends time. How often has God heard us grumbling and murmuring on our way to a proffered blessing—as if we were doing Him a favor? And if we were more honest with ourselves as well as with Him, how many times have we, later on, in the quietude of reflection given silent thanks for His seeming interference with our schedule? Some apparent interventions are actually required to get us back on our real schedule!

Too often we construe *faith* in the Lord to mean only acceptance of His existence, an acknowledgment that He is there. What is wanted, since He is there, is our *trust* of Him, including His plans for us. Let us not complain of large classes in this mortal school when, at the same time, we consistently decline His offers to tutor us privately!

The surprising thing is that we are so often taken in by transitory considerations. Perhaps we think all the human huckstering is done by comparatively harmless confidence men. Careless mortal grants of amnesty and pardons to criminals do not mirror either divine mercy or divine justice; these are not to be confused with His day of reckoning.

However, some may nevertheless be counting on God's generosity toward our "little sins," after which indulgence we are beaten with a few stripes and then are saved in the kingdom of God. (2 Nephi 28:8.) The naiveté—"and if it so be that we are guilty"—rests on a doubt that God is really serious about our keeping His commandments. What a gross misreading of the nature of God! For those who make this tragic error and think their Father to be an indulgent father, it is no wonder they themselves do not wax serious about developing the eternal attributes in their own lives. Such naiveté fosters false religion, as Bagehot observed:

> But the *attractive* aspects of God's character must not be made more apparent to such a being as man than his chastening and severer aspects; we must not be invited to approach the Holy of Holies without being made aware, painfully aware, what holiness is; we must know our own unworthiness ere we are fit to approach or imagine an infinite Perfection. The most nauseous of false religions is that which affects a fulsome fondness for a Being not to be thought of without awe or spoken of without reluctance.[20]

It is the first order of a true religion to understand the nature of God. Then it is possible to understand life and ourselves and what it is we are here to do.

Life really becomes better only when we become better. The diversions and the illusions are such that, unless we are very careful, we will be diverted. Life unfolds only as we unfold spiritually. It is the world that is always closing us down, as when sin scalds the tastebuds of the soul and we lose our appetite for true sweetness.

The desired eternal attributes and everlasting skills can be—and, of course, are—developed while seriously pursuing different mortal tasks. A statesman can be growing in his patience as well as in his skills of diplomacy. A watch repairman may be increasing in his capacity to use time wisely and not just his ability to help watches keep time. The problem is not usually that our mortal tasks are irrelevant, but that these can become consuming ends in themselves, diversions that keep us from our appointed roles and our real tasks.

It would strike us as odd, for instance, if we attended the theater and found, as soon as the performers came on stage, that they quickly lost interest in why they were there and in the other players. We would think an actor quite irresponsible if, instead of proceeding with his performance, he suddenly became fascinated with the scenery to the neglect of other performers or the audience, or if an actress became totally obsessed with what was in the fruit bowl rather than carrying out her part and uttering her lines.

But is this not what happens all the time on the stage of life? Some conclude, for instance, that they have come here to acquire money, not the eternal attributes. Others can hardly wait for the curtain to rise so they can garner the praise of men. They miss what is really supposed to be going on.

When life is viewed superficially, however, it may seem to be all routine and incurably pedestrian. Cynics even speak of birth, marriage, and death as the "hatch-match-and-dispatch" dimension of life. However, what appears to be mere humdrum on the surface can be a thin cover for what is really underway.

So it is that when looking only at the surface of their lives, some may say, "Is this all my life is to be?" If what is meant by the question is, "Can I become better and do more?," the answer is a definite "Yes!" If, however, the question is meant to imply that the essential drama or significance of life is missing, then the answer is definitely "No!" In a very real way, what life is all about is the development of the eternal attributes and everlasting skills. All else is ancillary.

It is not merely amusing but absurd when people get so caught up with the props and scenery in life to the neglect of what they have come here for. Years ago, some who were young joined the French Foreign Legion in search of adventure. The Lord, in fact, is trying to spare us such dullness. What He offers us is real adventure—a "battlefield commission" in His royal army.

In those two episodes when whole peoples enjoyed great spiritual outcomes as a result of righteousness, they were described as being free of lyings, tumults, and whoredoms or any manner of sexual immorality. They were also described as being happy, as sharing their economic wealth, and as being of one heart. (See 4 Nephi; Moses 7:18.) Yes, they also married and were given in marriage; they fasted, prayed, and met together often. (4 Nephi 1:11-12.) Note how familiar the surface seems—but what uncommon outcomes!

We do not read of Enoch's or Nephi's people that their gross national product went up seventy percent, that they achieved a more favorable balance of trade, that their legislative bodies passed a record number of bills. Does it really matter much now, for instance, that Mussolini, who never did understand the efficiency of freedom, made the trains run on time? And how important a skill will "making the trains run on time" be in a trainless world?

These eternal attributes are not entirely otherworldly. How much human history would be strikingly different if these attributes were more valued now? How many "unconditional surrenders" have spawned more war because vengeance, not mercy, prevailed? And how many solutions to society's complex problems go unreached because the search for vindication takes preeminence over communication, or militancy over meekness?

Because looking at life and others through the lens of the gospel provides eternal perspective, if we look long enough, as well as often enough, we can see much more clearly and also measure the size of things. Such things as a mess of pottage and thirty pieces of silver and moments of sensual pleasure totally disappear from view; so does an improved golf swing or tennis serve when compared with progress toward patience. So does redecorating the front room when placed alongside listening and teaching one's children.

Superficial assessments of things are apt to miss the mark. Man's logic is, after all, demonstrably finite. Stranded mountain climbers might need to go just a bit higher in order to get down safely. Surgery that momentarily produces pain may be necessary in order to relieve pain; open heart surgery virtually stops the natural movement of the heart in order to improve the natural movement of the heart.

What we see and think can be quite provincial. This is where the trust in God comes in. And why should we not encounter certain experiences that require us to trustingly strike balances? Can we help His cause as much if we do not understand both the need for and the risks of self-denial lest it become mere asceticism? Can we be as useful to Him if we do not strike balances between improper pride and self-flagellation? After all, if we are to esteem and love our neighbors as ourselves, does this not underscore the need for healthy self-esteem and self-regard?

Finally, the eternal virtues and attributes are not

useful to discuss apart from Him. Submissiveness to Him—as a child doth submit to his father—is both safe and necessary. Indeed, it is the only way that He, in His perfect love, can tutor us. But submissiveness to an errant individual is not humility. Patience in the framework of His purposes is vital—but patience would quickly become indulgence in a setting in which a parent's child abuse goes unchecked again and again.

He is at the center of it all! It is He (and His plan) who keeps the balance as well as provides the *raison d'etre* for it all. So it is that when some speak of morality apart from God, it makes little sense, for there can be no ordering principles without an Orderer.

In a very real way, as we think upon Him, it becomes clear that not only when we contemplate the galaxies do we see God "moving in his majesty and power" (D&C 88:47), but we also see Him "moving in his majesty and power" when we see a soul who was once belligerent and is now moving toward meekness, and a soul who was once no more than a bundle of appetites and is now increasingly full of love toward God and man. After all, is such transformation not what He said His work is all about?

Chapter Five

"Summer Is Nigh"
(Matthew 24:32)

After the Savior had spoken of some of the specific signs of His second coming, He gave to His disciples, and to us all, the parable of the fig tree. When the fig tree puts forth its leaves, He said, we may know that "summer is nigh." Similarly, we may be warned by certain accumulating signs that His second coming is nigh. (Matthew 24:32-33.) The "summer" Jesus cited is upon us. We must neither complain of the heat nor let that heat, as Alma counseled, wither our individual tree of testimony, because we will surely feel the heat of that summer sun in our individual lives as the prophesied developments occur on this planet.

Underlying conditions will produce some of the signs and indicators. The prophets speak, for instance, of the last days as being a time when people will be selfish, "lovers of their own selves" (2 Timothy 3:2), a "culture of narcissism." The last days will also be an age when "the love of many shall wax cold." (Matthew 24:12; D&C 45:27.)

Out of such basic deficiencies, the cataclysm of war will arise. Peacemaking processes inevitably break down as the lubricant of love becomes more and more rare, as coarseness replaces meekness, and as confrontation replaces patience.

Another bedrock sign is that "all things shall be in commotion." (D&C 88:91; 45:26; Luke 21:9.) Commotion is defined as civil unrest, agitation, disorder, and insurrection. Political commotions grow out of the underlying unrighteousness, discord, and confusion over what are to be society's basic and ordering values. Malcolm Muggeridge wrote of today's "tragi-comic spectacle" of secularism in which

illiteracy increases along with expenditure on public education, the demand for sedatives with increased leisure or affluence, and crimes of violence (particularly rape) with libertarian schemes to prevent them and rehabilitate their perpetrators. The more pacifists and internationalists in the world, the more belligerency; the more free speech, the less truth spoken; the more maternal and child care, the more fetuses aborted and thrown away with the hospital waste. Oh, the terrible unhumanity of the humane, the fathomless gullibility of the enlightened! the relentless egoism of the well-intentioned![21]

The last days are also times when "men's hearts shall fail them." (D&C 45:26; D&C 88:91.) The Lord placed, as a "pearl of great price," an insight into this condition that says: "But before that day he saw great tribulations among the wicked; and he also saw the sea, that it was troubled, and men's hearts failing them, *looking forth with fear for the judgments of the Almighty God*, which should come upon the wicked." (Moses 7:66. Italics added.)

Apparently some of the fear that will envelop modern mankind will not be agnostic fear alone, but old-fashioned fear and foreboding over the impending "judgments of the Almighty God." Walter Bagehot described a dimension of this fearfulness of the faithless:

They are fearful of future punishment, because some Being in the air has threatened it. They have not the true belief in the Divine holiness which arises from a love of holiness; they have not the true conception of God which was suggested by conscience and is kept alive by the activity of conscience: but they have a vague persuasion that a great Personage has asserted this, and why they should believe that Personage they do not ask or know.[22]

But even in the midst of such commotions, some will persist in their valiant search for truth, and for the deepest of reasons:

. . . the heaving of the mind after the truth [when] troubled with the perplexities of time, weary with the vexation of ages, the spiritual faculty of man turns to the truth as the child turns to its mother. The thirst of the soul was to be satisfied, the deep torture of the spirit to have rest.[23]

Conditions before Jesus' second coming, we are further told, will resemble those in the days of Noah when there was a misdirected sense of self-sufficiency among the citizenry, a resistance to the words of the Lord's prophet, and a dangerous norm of wickedness as usual. The attitudes among some latter-day scoffers will reflect the same scornful self-sufficiency. Even the unmistakable signs will be discounted, because, said Peter, such people will say "all things continue as they were." (2 Peter 3:3-4.) Joseph Smith, in the inspired translation of the Bible, added, significantly, that these same latter-day scoffers would also deny the divinity of the Lord Jesus Christ, a sad reality that is well advanced even now. G. K. Chesterton has pointed out that when people cease to believe in God, instead of believing in nothing, what is far more dangerous is that they believe in anything.

Alexander Solzhenitsyn has perceptively said:

We are approaching a major turning point in world history, in the history of civilization. . . . It is a juncture at which settled concepts suddenly become hazy, lose their precise contours. . . . It's the sort of turning point where the hierarchy of values which we have venerated, and which we use to determine what is important to us and what causes our hearts to beat is starting to rock and may collapse.[24]

There will be those in our time, too, who will say of the clearly fulfilled prophecies of the Lord's anointed that the true prophets simply "guessed right, among so many" prophecies. (Helaman 16:16.) Because "summer is nigh," however, do we cease all regular activities? No, we pursue life's goals but with added awareness and with the Holy Spirit as our guide.

Since space does not permit an assessment of all accumulating signs, let a brief discussion of education serve as but one sample of some of the drift and difficulties in the modern world even though education is to be pursued in both the heat and the opportunities that make up this summer.

In the midst of the gathering storm in the fall of 1939, C. S. Lewis spoke to students and scholars at Oxford of continuing the quest for knowledge, saying:

If men had postponed the search for knowledge and beauty until they were secure, the search would never have begun. . . . Life has never been normal. . . . Humanity . . . wanted knowledge and beauty now, and would not wait for the suitable moment that never comes. . . . The insects have chosen a different line: they have sought first the material welfare and security of the hive, and presumably they have their reward. Men are different. They propound mathematical theorems in beleaguered cities, conduct metaphysical arguments in condemned cells, make jokes on scaffolds, discuss the latest new poem while advancing to the walls of Quebec, and comb their hair at Thermopylae. This is not *panache*: it is our nature.[25]

The same perspective about the pursuit of knowledge and beauty must be ours in this final summer. But the goal should be "knowledge with Godliness."

The early universities (Paris, Bologna, Oxford, Cambridge, and Harvard) had Christian religion at their core. The University of Paris, for instance, stood at the heart of the spiritual life of its age, but such universities, wrote Richard Hofstadter, "were scarcely less important as agencies of practical life, whose work was as relevant to the ecclesiastical and political life of the thirteenth and fourteenth centuries as the modern university is to the scientific and industrial life of our time."[26]

The 1650 charter for Harvard College spoke of "the advancement of all good literature, artes and Sciences," "*in knowledge: and godliness.*"[27]

Edward Reynolds, a Puritan author, correctly observed:

All truth must by definition come from God, and all knowledge of truth be ultimately knowledge of Him; but we must recognize that "there is a knowledge of God *natural* in and by *his works* and a knowledge *supernatural* by revelation out of the Word; and though this be the principal, yet the other is not to be undervalued."[28]

Reynolds also wrote affirmatively of such education and how "*Sanctified Wit* beautifies Religion, sanctified *Reason* defends it, sanctified *power* protects it, sanctified *Elocution* perswades others to the love of it."[29]

Many once church-related institutions, however, have long since become indistinguishable from other universities and colleges, keeping the ceremonial robes without the theology, the pomp without the purpose.

As the contest intensifies in this final summer, education is in the center of the fray as to what are and are not the basic beliefs at the center of it all. Secularists appear to be carrying the day, often because they go unchallenged as they break with tradition. We are all "free to choose," including educators, but the consequences of our choices will be felt, and this is the case in education, for there are no immunities from the consequences of our choices.

Those who foolishly assert that there is no God, no absolute truths, and no divine design in the universe have sown the wind and reaped the whirlwinds in education.

The attempts to inculcate morality independent of religion are like the actions of children who, wishing to move a plant which pleases them, tear off the root which does not please, and seems unnecessary to them, and plant it in the earth without the root. Without a religious foundation there can be no true, sincere morality, as without a root there can be no true plant.[30]

So it is that:

A child starting school in America in the 1980s can now begin his education with "instruction" in values-clarification at the elementary level, wherein he will learn 'that there is no right and wrong' and that 'life is a lovely banquet' in which he can take what he likes. Then he can go on to high school and engage in "cognitive moral development" where he will learn to question all forms of authority, particularly that of the family, whose "conditioning," as this report calls it, he will learn to recognize for what it is. From there, he can go on to college where he will learn to question the "permanent validity" of American cultural ideals—that is, if he has even heard of them.[31]

The trend has been underway for many years:

The Thomas Jefferson Research Center, a nonprofit institution studying America's social problems, reports that in 1775, religion and morals accounted for more than 90 percent of the content of school readers. By 1926 the figure was only 6 percent. Today it is almost nonexistent. A study of third grade readers reported that references to obedience, thoughtfulness and honesty began to disappear after 1930.[32]

How dramatic the departure from our roots as the scorching sun of secularism dries up the heritage of the past!

Surely education and existentialism qualify as one of history's oddest couples. If there is no discernible purpose for man in the universe, how purposeful is education? Can education be a hopeful enterprise if man's circumstance is, at bottom, hopeless? If life is absurd and unexplainable, can education lay legitimate claim to society's resources for the purpose of articulating absurdity or explaining the unexplainable?

How much need there is in education (as in so many other sectors) for articulating basic gospel truths and for giving reasons underlying the hope that is in us (1 Peter 3:15)—but in meekness.

Religious and moral values were so essential to America in its beginnings. They are no less so now. George Washington, in his farewell address, warned:

Of all the dispositions and habits which lead to political prosperity, religion and morality are indispensable supports. . . . let us with caution indulge the supposition that morality can be maintained without religion. Whatever may be conceded to the influence of refined education on minds of peculiar structure, reason and experience both forbid us to expect that national morality can prevail in exclusion of religious principle.[33]

Can educators speak with a solemn and straight face about discovering and preserving truth if there is no truth? Or are there only truths pertaining to physical nature but none pertaining to human nature? And if so, where did the former come from? Do not efforts to infuse education with relativism, which rejects the reality of existence of absolute truths, therefore contain an incredible irony and, in fact, sow the seeds of self-destruction?

Ortega y Gasset said of relativism's fatal flaw: "If truth does not exist, relativism cannot take itself seriously. . . . belief in truth is a deeply-rooted foundation of human life; if we remove it, life is converted into an illusion and an absurdity."[34]

More poetically, Alexander Pope wrote of what happens without belief in a Creator: "Philosophy, that lean'd on Heaven before/Shrinks to her second cause, and is no more."[35]

The gospel, however, advises us that when we are serious scholars and students, we are actually about our Father's business. Indeed, as George MacDonald observed: "Human science is but the backward undoing of the tapestry-web of God's science."[36]

Secularized education, on the other hand, when it is disdainful of things spiritual, cannot deliver on the bright hopes for education's role such as those of Horace Mann, who said:

Let the common school be expanded to its capabilities, . . . and nine-tenths of the crimes in the penal code will become obsolete; the lone catalogue of human ills will be abridged; men will walk more safely by day; every pillow will be more inviolable by night; property, life, and character will be held by a stronger tenure; all rational hopes reflecting the future brightened.[37]

Without moral content, however, can public education really produce public safety? Can love of culture by itself save mankind if we do not first love God enough to keep His commandments? Can the love of great music ensure the love of one's neighbor? After all, did not Adolf Eichmann watch the torching of Jews in "the crematoria to the strains of Haydn"?[38]

No wonder that the Church must be a sanctuary amid the barren wilderness of secularism!

Alexis de Tocqueville, who foresaw the alienation of many Americans, used these words to portray the shrinking circles of concern, words that might well be used to describe secularized men and women:

> They owe nothing to any man, they expect nothing from any man; they acquire the habit of always considering themselves as standing alone, and they are apt to imagine that their whole destiny is in their own hands.
>
> Thus not only does democracy make every man forget his ancestors, but it hides his descendants and separates his contemporaries from him; it throws him back forever upon himself alone and threatens in the end to confine him entirely within the solitude of his own heart.[39]

What a stark contrast to those who seriously, though imperfectly, pursue the second great commandment!

Happily, both true education and true religion help us to distinguish between trivial truths and eternal truths, as well as between sense and nonsense. The disciple-scholar who is grounded, rooted, established, and settled will surmount the challenge of secularism in this summer of secularism. He will know which kind of truth it is that makes us free.

There is a hierarchy of truth atop which are the great ordering realities: the reality of Deity, the reality of immortality, and the reality of an eternal ecology that rests upon God's commandments. When Jesus of Nazareth spoke of how the truth can make us free, He was not speaking of those facts contained in today's principles of accounting class or of data concerning crop yields, but of these great emancipating truths, which are everlasting and not ephemeral.

These great truths constitute the common ground upon which so many mortals stand together, almost without realizing it—a shared belief in God and in a purposeful mortal existence, with human happiness being determined by our capacity to keep God's commandments. Besides, if there are no overarching truths in the universe, then are not all facts equal, and is not information synonymous with wisdom? It was T. S. Eliot who asked searchingly: "Where is the wisdom we have lost in knowledge, where is the knowledge we have lost in information?"[40]

The author of Proverbs wisely said, "The commandment is a lamp." (Proverbs 6:23.) Once mortals depart from that light, then the shadows lengthen, and behavior that was prohibited becomes permitted. The efforts of secular societies to balance liberty and order otherwise will finally fail, for the light from the lamps of the Lord is not just something we can see—it is the light by means of which we see everything else, especially how we see ourselves and our situation.

These lamps of the Lord not only help us to see who we are, but also illuminate the lessons of the past. Cardinal Newman described a superior intellect as "one which takes a connected view of old and new, past and present, far and near, and which has an insight into the influences of all these one on another."[41] Truth, after all, involves "knowledge of things as they *are*, and as they *were*, and as they are *to come*." (D&C 93:24. Italics added.) President Charles W. Penrose put it well:

Truth does not change with the centuries. It will not change with the eternal ages. The truth of God abideth forever. That which is true, coming from Him in one age of the world, is true in another. [D&C 93:24-25.] That which is true on one of His worlds that He has created, is true in all the worlds that He has caused to be organized and sent forth, each in its place, rolling in space, revolving upon its own axis, preserved in its own sphere, in its own orbit, and with the others contributing to the glory of God and bespeaking His handiwork. Truth never changes. Our conception of a truth may change as we grow in wisdom and understanding, and in clearness of spiritual vision. That which appeared to us to be true at one time we may find out later to be incorrect, and so it is we who change, and not the truth that changes.[42]

With illumination comes a true sense of proportion that enables us to study the present while being tutored by the past. Proportion keeps us from exclaiming over trivia, whether new or old. Scholars who pour over ancient clay tablets need that sense of proportion lest they exclaim over inscribings that were long ago merely a cargo list, while ignoring the Sermon on the Mount. Futurists need proportion lest they exult over how technology can bring us ease and luxury, but without remembering what history sternly tells us about some of the consequences of too much ease and luxury.

Proportion is what Paul wrote about when he said the true disciple who is "rooted and grounded in love" is then "able to comprehend . . . what is the breadth, and length, and depth, and height." (Ephesians 3:17-18.) Another prophet, Jacob, spoke of how God can add to our understanding by teaching us of "things as they really are, and of things as they really will be." (Jacob 4:13.)

Some disbelievers do not necessarily deny the great truths but are simply too preoccupied with other concerns.

They do not deny them, but they live apart from them; they do not disbelieve them, but they are silent when they are stated. They do not question the existence of Kamtchatka, but they have no call to busy themselves with Kamtchatka; they abstain from peculiar tenets. Nor in truth is this, though much aggravated by existing facts, a mere accident of this age,—there are some people to whom such a course of conduct is always natural: there are certain persons who do not, as it would seem cannot, feel all that others feel; who have, so to say no *ear* for much of religion,—who are in some sort out of its reach.[43]

Is there a remedy?

If you could extend before men the awful vision of everlasting perdition; if they could see it as they see the things of earth,—as they see Fleet Street and St. Paul's; if you could show men likewise the inciting vision of an everlasting heaven, if they could see that too with undeniable certainty and invincible distinctness,— who could say that they would have a thought for any other motive?[44]

Again, how great the challenge of articulation as we poor preachers seek to portray the basic gospel message to near-believers and disbelievers alike!

When we read such scriptures as "my ways [are] higher than your ways" (Isaiah 55:9); "the wisdom of this world is foolishness with God" (1 Corinthians 3:19); and that learning "is good if [we] hearken unto the counsels of God" (2 Nephi 9:29)—are not those precisely the kinds of cautions and instructions that would come from an omniscient but beckoning God to stumbling, shortsighted, provincial humans? And do not the meek understand?

George MacDonald noted man's perceptual and conceptual limitations when he aptly declared that "the miracles of Jesus were the ordinary works of His Father, wrought small and swift that we might take them in."[45]

No wonder G. K. Chesterton tartly observed, "Men will not believe because they will not broaden their minds."[46]

Moreover, it should be quickly added, divine instructions such as "study it out in your mind" (D&C 9:8) did not come from a God indifferent to the intellect. Multiple counsel to "ponder" things did not come from a God mistrustful of the mind.

In sum, concerning the status of education as but one indicator in this final summer, it must be said that to be learned *is* good, but only if we do not become so proud of our newly acquired capacity to manage the multiplication tables that we refuse to consider the challenge of calculus.

To be poorly educated academically is a disadvantage. To be poorly educated in the things of the Spirit is tragedy. It is one thing to misread life and its purposes and quite another to split one's infinitives.

If there is no solution to the human predicament, as secular pessimists say, can there be any solutions to mankind's tactical problems? And from what base point do we proceed in order to be consistent? Is a population explosion wrong, for instance, but a copulation explosion all right?

In the search for peace, can we ask for God's help in rallying the human family to avoid a nuclear holocaust, if we neglect the nuclear family wherein we can learn, first and best, about love, taking turns, negotiating, and restraining selfishness? Should some cite failing fathers as cause to abandon the institution of the family, note Joseph Sobran's usual, uncommon sense:

. . . the autocracy of the father was a natural check on the autocracy of the king. There have always been bad fathers, but the average of fathers, on the whole, is higher than that of kings: affection is a surer protection than the love of justice. Besides it is easier to flee a father than an empire. In the era of patriarchy people had much less to fear from state power than they do now.[47]

How much sustained attention to civic duty will there be without the foundation of a prior regard for the duties that flow from the first and second great commandments? Otherwise, the growing narcissism, adulation, and worship of self, fostered by relativism, will mock the attempts to deal with mankind's increasing interdependency.

How much sense of personal responsibility will

there finally be for many individuals who do not believe in their ultimate accountability to God? And how long can we keep the culture of service alive in the acid of secular selfishness? How much environmental deference will there be for those of tomorrow without belief in the everlasting tomorrow of immortality?

Can man's sense of stewardship for this planet be sustained if it is not, ultimately, a stewardship for and in behalf of a loving God? We can scarcely persuade some today to assume responsibility for their aging parents, let alone feel responsible for generations unborn, unknown, and unseen!

How much real justice or mercy will there be without that love which is the centerpiece of the first and second great commandments? Without love, said George MacDonald, "we can no more render justice than a man can keep a straight line, walking in the dark."[48]

How much real respect will there be between the generations unless we obey the fifth commandment by honoring our earthly parents? Perhaps it was inevitable that those in society who ceased to honor their fathers and mothers would next view husbands, wives, and children as disposable. Is there not a connection between our failure to acknowledge God, whose spirit sons and daughters we are, and the failure to keep the fifth commandment?

And how much interpersonal integrity will there be without our also keeping the seventh commandment with its requirement of fidelity and integrity within the marriage covenant? The very essence of integrity insists that it cannot be a compartmentalized or an episodic thing.

How much genuine political or economic tranquillity will there be if we do not obey the tenth commandment and forgo coveting? Envy is still envy even when it is politicized and legalized.

And how much collegiality and neighborliness will there be unless we keep the ninth commandment by refusing to bear false witness and by insisting on fair play one with another? Such empathy and concern as are needed to cope with human interdependence do not arise out of mere biological brotherhood.

Of course, a loving God, deeply committed to free agency, has left mankind free to reject and to violate His commandments. But there are no secular substitutes! The seventh commandment does not read, for instance, "Thou shalt not commit adultery except between consenting adults." Nor does it read "Thou shalt not commit adultery unless it is in a 'meaningful relationship.' "

A narcissistic society in which each person is too busy looking out for "number one" can build no brotherhood; it will finally be shattered against its own selfishness. Had God's Firstborn looked out for Himself first, there would have been no Gethsemane or Calvary— and no immortality!

Secular standards so often constitute a naive Maginot-line morality that is quickly outflanked by the reality of what occurs when men and women try to live without God in the world. Over four decades ago, the lights began to go out all over Europe. Extinguished were the lamps of God's commandments, including the sixth commandment. In the resulting darkness, the genocide of millions of Jews occurred.

The greater the darkness, the more enormous the errors. In that darkness, some said they did not know about concentration camps; the darkness made it easier for others who did know to ignore what was underway. The time may well come when the enormity of widespread and unnecessary abortions of today (one legal abortion for every three live births in the United States in 1978) will be looked upon with at least some of the shame with which we now view Dachau and Buchenwald.

Though parallels between periods of time are seldom perfect, history is not really as silent as we are sometimes deaf. This last summer and its happenings can be better understood if we look back—beyond Buchenwald and more distantly than Dachau—to Rome, of which Will Durant wrote:

The virile character that had been formed by arduous simplicities and a supporting faith relaxed in the sunshine of wealth and the freedom of unbelief; men had now, in the middle and upper classes, the means to yield to temptation, and only expediency to restrain them. Urban congestion multiplied contacts and frustrated surveillance; immigration brought together a hundred cultures whose differences rubbed themselves out into indifference. Moral and esthetic standards were lowered by the magnetism of the mass; and sex ran riot in freedom while political liberty decayed.[49]

And of the same Rome, Aaron Stern wrote:

The Roman Empire provides a richly detailed description of the decline of a great society. The symptoms of its fall centered around a critical schism between the older and younger generations. It was reflected among the young by an increase in drug usage, by a growing experimentation in homosexuality and bisexuality, and, perhaps most symptomatic of all, by a strident demand for more leisure that was accompanied by an unwillingness to accept responsibility for government, family, and other institutions.[50]

The anxiousness and the effectiveness of the adversary will also be in evidence in this final summer. Since he cannot put down gospel truths *per se*, the adversary seems capable of showcasing examples of these correct principles gone wild. Error coated with truth has ever been his tactic, and the thicker the coating the better. He uses the perversion of a principle as an argument against that principle—lust parading as love as an argument against love, the dole to stifle generosity, pride to mock genuine self-esteem, cowardice to masquerade as meekness, and apathy pretending to be patience.

Again, harking backing to the basic truths about life—since we are here to be proved and to grow "in process of time," selfishness is something to be overcome, not something to be asserted. Surely our real individuality is more than a particular configuration of selfish needs with which we assault a spouse, siblings, fellow-workers, or society!

Many, for instance, enter marriage blithely thinking that they will stay wed only as long as *their* needs are met. No mention is made of the role of sacrifice, as if life were all receiving and no giving, and as if mere reciprocity, instead of generosity, were the ultimate standard.

The apostate notion of fulfillment has held sway for some years now, captivating not only the uninitiated but even the veterans if they straggle or stray. Self-pity comes so easily to most of us; it takes so little to call it forth. And life is such that most days contain within them seeming excuses for being piqued. It is such a small step from self-pity to becoming offended.

That we so often harvest where we have not sown, that we venerate unselfish women and men who have given something special to society, that materialism has, again and again, demonstrated its emptiness—these self-evident truths do not seem to count. No wonder! When the addiction to selfishness has reached a certain stage, the darkness is thick. It is difficult to ask the alcoholic to put a filled tumbler down.

No use asking one whose only criterion is "ME" to suddenly wax democratic in his concerns. For some, self-restraint is viewed as but a quaint concept.

How did it all happen? There are so many reasons.

Arianna Stassinopoulous, former president of the Cambridge Union, wrote recently: "The relegation of religion and spirituality to the irrational has been one of the most tragic perversions of the great achievements of Western Rationality, and the main reason for the disintegration of Western Culture."[51]

How pervasive the challenge, therefore, to those who are grounded, rooted, established, and settled, especially in preserving and nourishing the family. Michael Novak noted in *Harper's*:

> The family nourishes "basic trust." From this spring creativity, psychic energy, social dynamism. If infants are injured here, not all the institutions of society can put them back together. Familial strength that took generations to acquire can be lost in a single generation, can disappear for centuries. If the quality of family life deteriorates, there is no "quality of life."[52]

How real the need to preserve intact families as well as improve them!

If one ever wondered at the seeming rapidity with which social, economic, and political changes occurred during the millennium of Book of Mormon history, this observation by Alberta Siegel is worth remembering: "Every civilization is only 20 years away from barbarism. For 20 years is all we have to accomplish the task of civilizing the infants . . . who know nothing of our language, our culture, our religion, our values, or our customs of interpersonal relations."[53]

But is not secularism often sincere? Yes, but suppose someone had installed suggestion boxes on the last day on the job at the construction site of the Tower of Babel! Would his sincerity have mattered much?

If one thinks about it at all, it becomes quickly and abundantly clear that the differing assumptions about the nature of man, the purpose of life, and the nature of God will produce polarization.

True, much of society once shared approximately the same assumptions about God and life with resulting traditional values. True, also, that many who are not outspoken still cling to those traditional assumptions. But alas, departures from traditional values concerning the role of the family—what is and what is not sin, one's duties to God and to his fellowmen—lead to a growing divergence. Regrettable as this is, it is.

Those who are intent on building the secular City of Man will be increasingly impatient with those who build the City of God! Brotherhood pursued in such circumstances is a real test of our love as well as of our capacity to articulate. But so it is.

In challenging the onrushing hedonism or preoccupation with pleasure and secularism of our time, we can be pardoned a certain shivering of the soul as we contemplate that which waits to be done in the world. But secularism is not irreversible.

Let us respect the rights of those who sincerely believe that man is alone and appreciate their personal decency, which so often is in evidence. But shall we let their conclusions be automatically translated into pervasive public policies? There should be neither a state religion nor a state irreligion.

We can be humble without being mute, and effective without being strident. Men and women of religion need not be silent when governments try to redefine morality. Believers need not be docilely confined to the catacombs.

Let us be good neighbors. Let us be quietly about our Father's business even if some do not believe there is a Father. We should respect the freedoms of those who perform their oblations only in the temple of time; they may find it necessary, however, to be quick about their rituals and to burn their candles briskly, for eternity is closing in!

Let us be persons of good works and good will, cultivating a sense of humor that allows for our critics. Believers may smile at times when disbelievers seem to be like the two goldfish debating in the fishbowl with one saying to the other, "Well, if there is no God, who changes the water?"

The summer clearly calls for the spunk of Winston Churchill, who in embattled England's darkest days took himself up to Harrow School and said: "Do not let us speak of darker days; let us speak rather of sterner days. These are not dark days: these are great days—the greatest days our country has ever lived; and we must all thank God that we have been allowed, each of us according to our stations, to play a part in making these days memorable in the history of our race."[54]

Let us give a good account of ourselves in these sterner days. We can make a difference. Let us so live and serve as to give no one just cause to speak spitefully of us. People may say untrue things that hurt. But let us so serve that those who are unrighteous, as Paul counseled, "may be ashamed, having no evil thing to say of you." (Titus 2:8.)

One can see why successive Church leaders have construed the parable of the ten virgins to apply with particularity to the members of The Church of Jesus Christ of Latter-day Saints in the final summer.

"And at that day, when I shall come in my glory, shall the parable be fulfilled which I spake concerning the ten virgins.

97

"For they that are wise and have received the truth, and have taken the Holy Spirit for their guide, and have not been deceived—verily I say unto you, they shall not be hewn down and cast into the fire, but shall abide the day." (D&C 45:56-57.)

President Harold B. Lee indicated that those foolish virgins in the parable could be likened unto those who would be cut off from the Church.[55]

"And the arm of the Lord shall be revealed; and the day cometh that they who will not hear the voice of the Lord, neither the voice of his servants, neither give heed to the words of the prophets and apostles, shall be cut off from among the people;

"For they have strayed from mine ordinances, and have broken mine everlasting covenant." (D&C 1:14-15.)

Thus we see how the parable applies to the people of God who foolishly neglect their duties; there will be a separation among professing believers.

Elder James E. Talmage links the Parable of the Ten Virgins with the Parable of the Sower, wherein the Savior tells about how the gospel seed fell, some of it on stony fields, and took no root and withered.[56] The wise are those who have received the truth, who have taken the Holy Spirit for their guide, and who have not been deceived. But there will not be an entire separation of the righteous and the wicked until that time:

"These things are the things that ye must look for; and speaking after the manner of the Lord, they are now nigh at hand, and in a time to come, even in the day of the coming of the Son of Man.

"And until that hour there will be foolish virgins among the wise; and at that hour cometh an entire separation of the righteous and the wicked; and in that day will I send mine angels to pluck out the wicked and cast them into unquenchable fire." (D&C 63:53-54.)

The summer is taking its toll. But even in the heat of the final summer, we can come to know the deep reassurance that Paul described when he said, "We are troubled on every side, yet not distressed; we are perplexed, but not in despair; persecuted, but not forsaken; cast down, but not destroyed." (2 Corinthians 4:8-9.) Why? Because we are grounded, rooted, established, and settled. We can be in withering circumstances and yet not wither. We can endure the heat of that special summer.

Chapter Six

"Unwearied Diligence"
(Helaman 15:6)

Few balances are more difficult to strike than achieving equipoise between the counsel of the Lord to guard against running faster than we have strength and means (Mosiah 4:27; D&C 10:4), and His counsel to display "unwearied diligence" in our discipleship (Helaman 15:6).

It would be both foolish and untrue to suggest that discipleship is free of physical fatigue—clearly it is not. There *are* unmistakable times when "the spirit indeed is willing, but the flesh is weak." (Matthew 26:41.) However, part of enduring well to the end includes moving forward even when we are truly physically fatigued. Even so, it includes as well those moments when the need for renewal through rest, repose, or respite calls for "sacred idleness."

Since the Lord would give us neither contradictory counsel nor impossible commands, it is for us to strive for the needed balance. The search for this balance is clearly worth the effort, since it carries with it this glorious promise:

"Blessed art thou, Nephi, for those things which

thou hast done; for I have beheld how thou hast *with unwearyingness declared the word,* which I have given unto thee, unto this people. And thou hast not feared them, and hast not sought thine own life, but hast *sought my will,* and to keep my commandments.

"And now, because thou hast done this with such *unwearyingness,* behold, I will *bless thee forever;* and I will make thee *mighty in word and in deed, in faith and in works;* yea, even that all things shall be *done unto thee according to thy word,* for thou shalt not ask that which is contrary to my will." (Helaman 10:4-5. Italics added.)

Such steadfastness! Such selflessness! Such attunement to Divine will!

There is a phase line in our spiritual progress that, if crossed by means of "unwearied diligence" and righteousness, yields both renewal and reward. We will not even ask amiss in our petitions, and, therefore, our prayers will be granted even as we ask. (D&C 50:29-30; 46:30.) Others speak with justification of the efficiency of freedom, but we can also speak of the enormous efficiency of righteousness.

Successive, small, and connected steps can, with "unwearied diligence," finally bring us where we wish to go, for God "regards men not as they are merely, but as they shall be; not as they shall be merely, but as they are now growing, . . . toward that image after which He made them. . . . Therefore *a thousand stages, each in itself all but valueless, are of inestimable worth* as the necessary and *connected gradations* of an infinite progress."[57]

How vital it is that we patiently pursue His purposes for us! How necessary it is to allow for the advancement through accretion that occurs "in process of time"!

Clearly just as the accumulation of small things is, in fact, the foundation of the Lord's great work, so also are the small steps that bring great blessings. The Lord has both tenderly and encouragingly reminded us of the following: "Wherefore, be not weary in well-doing, for ye are laying the foundation of a great work. And out of small things proceedeth that which is great." This invitation from the Lord to trust Him enough to give Him our heart and our mind obediently should stir us to acceptance. (D&C 64:33-34.)

But is there no immediate relief for weariness in well-doing? Are all the promises prospective?

"And any man that shall go and preach this gospel of the kingdom, and fail not to continue faithful in all things, *shall not be weary in mind*. . . . And they shall *not go hungry, neither athirst*." (D&C 84:80. Italics added.)

"For whoso is *faithful* unto the obtaining these two priesthoods of which I have spoken, *and the magnifying their calling*, are sanctified by the Spirit unto the *renewing of their bodies*." (D&C 84:33. Italics added.)

As we renew our efforts for Him, we are not only renewed in body, but we also avoid weariness of mind. One wonders just how much of our physical weariness is accounted for in our weariness of mind. Clearly atrophy in our attitudes precedes our spiritual slackness.

The Lord promises us relief from both forms of weariness if we will but trust Him—as do the lilies of the field: "Teach them to never be weary of good works, but to be meek and lowly in heart; for such shall find rest to their souls." (Alma 37:34.) Besides, can any rest compare with deserved rest for the soul? And are we not glad that God does not grow weary of blessing us?

Actually, much of our weariness is self-induced.

Some of us, for instance, ponder imponderables, adding to our weariness of mind. We fail to understand, as George MacDonald said, that "when we do not know, then what he lays upon us is *not to know.*"[58]

Some of us fret needlessly and unproductively, wearying ourselves with concerns that distract and divert us.

MacDonald also counseled regarding the tedium caused by trivia:

> We, too, dull our understandings with trifles, fill the heavenly space with phantoms, waste the heavenly time with hurry. When I trouble myself over a trifle, even a trifle confessed—the loss of some article, say—spurring my memory, and hunting the house, not from immediate need, but from dislike of loss; when a book has been borrowed of me and not returned, and I have forgotten the borrower, and fret over the missing volume . . . is it not time I lost a few things when I care for them so unreasonably? This losing of things is of the mercy of God: it comes to teach us to let them go. Or have I forgotten a thought that came to me, which seemed of the truth? . . . I keep trying and trying to call it back, feeling a poor man till that thought be recovered—to be far more lost, perhaps, in a notebook, into which I shall never look again to find it![59]

Some of our weariness comes from fussing over unessential things. "Seek ye first" leaves little room for the fussing that so often masquerades as conscientiousness.

True exhilaration, the incomparable antidote to weariness, comes from knowing and from conforming to our true identity and our true purposes on this planet. Purposelessness, however, brings a terrible weariness.

Meekness, one of the eternal attributes that is never obsolete and is portable, can help us achieve unwearyingness. The meek find rest to their souls because they do not always demand grand or immediate outcomes. They seek to serve rather than crave an enlarged impact. They are willing to contribute the alms of their activities without worrying about whether or not their almsgiving is visible. They are content to use the opportunities for service that are at hand instead of casting about for enlarged causes.

Furthermore, some of our fatigue, instead of being merely reduced, can be avoided altogether. We carry unnecessary burdens in our mortal luggage. While physical fatigue can often be dissolved after a good night's sleep, certain other causes of fatigue do not disappear so easily, as the following samples show.

Lies are wearying: "She hath wearied herself with lies. . . ." (Ezekiel 24:12.) So are the exacting mental computations that go with dissembling and the extra efforts required in the shading of the truth.

Hypocrisy is likewise a tremendous burden. It is such a fatiguing process to attempt to lead more than one life!

Vanity is a terrible taskmaster: "Behold, . . . the people shall weary themselves for very vanity." (Habakkuk 2:13.) Vanity is ever assertive, ever probing for every seeming possible advantage, ever alert for praise, and seldom sleeps; it precludes the self-knowledge required for eventual serenity.

Playing to the gallery in all its forms involves a wearying regimen. We cannot finally be concerned about pleasing Him if we are too concerned about pleasing *them*. Besides, playing to the roar of the crowd, be it a few peers or an imagined multitude, ends as an empty exercise. One realizes finally that he is in the wrong theater. We do well to let the bracing sea breeze of the scriptures clear our heads so far as the limitations and the risks of the praise of men are concerned.

What immense relief can also come from being freed by repentance from guilt. Indeed, though it is not always so, the immediacy with which some, when confronted, confess reflects the wearying burden that they now gladly begin to shed.

True, to live so as to please Him is a rigorous undertaking. But His burden is light compared to the burdens of sin, insincerity, vanity, and hypocrisy. His burden is bearable because, once we shoulder it and it alone, we can, mercifully, leave so much else behind.

Is there not also a refreshment that can come from righteous candor that seeks resolution? Yes, candor may create challenges. But candor focuses upon that which needs attention, and, if there is any mutual disposition to resolve, energies can then be expended wisely rather than being diffused—or, worse, reexpended again and again in brooding over an unnecessary frustration.

How often, too, do relationships drift into disrepair because of accumulating grievances, hardened by the passage of time and exaggerated by ego, that might be dissolved by loving candor? How simple and therapeutic is this counsel: "Moreover if thy brother shall trespass against thee, go and tell him his fault between thee and him alone: if he shall hear thee, thou hast gained thy brother." (Matthew 18:15.)

There is no guarantee that other individuals will respond when one attempts to end an impasse, but there is satisfaction in having genuinely tried to do one's own part; we can never do their part anyway.

To seek place above others is one of our greatest temptations; it is the most fatiguing form of climbing. William Law counseled:

The greatest trial of humility is a humble behavior towards your equals in age, state, and condition of life. Therefore be careful of all the motions of your heart towards these people. Let all your behavior towards them be governed by unfeigned love. Have no desire to put any of your equals below you, nor any anger at those who would put themselves above you. If they are proud, they are ill of a very bad distemper, let them therefore have your tender pity; and perhaps your meekness prove an occasion of their cure. But if your humility should do them no good, it will however be the greatest good that you can do to yourself.[60]

Law also observed how heroic that eternal attribute, humility, is:

Humility, which seems to be the lowest, meanest part of devotion, is a more certain argument of a noble and courageous mind. For humility contends with greater enemies, is more constantly engaged, more violently assaulted, bears more, suffers more, and requires greater courage to support itself, than any instances of worldly bravery.[61]

Besides, those who are rightly motivated will instinctively take their place at the foot of the banquet table, where they are able to enjoy both the company and the meal. There is no need for them to be distracted by watching for a chance to tablehop. One wonders how many meals sycophants and poseurs actually enjoy.

Additional weariness occurs because some of us bring such unrealistic expectations to life. All such unrealistic expectations about life are not merely amusing as is this one. George Knox, the father of the famous Bishop Knox of England, "had never looked up a train schedule in his life, but simply went down to the station and complained to the station-master if one was not ready for him."[62]

Few things weigh us down as does self-pity. Could Jesus on Calvary or Joseph Smith in Carthage have noticed others about them and comforted these if they had been preoccupied with self-pity?

Our daily chores go relentlessly on, but they need

not be amplified by the many burdens we need not carry. Some of us are so reluctant to let go of those needless bundles that they must almost be wrenched from our grasp.

How refreshing and necessary it is to have our priorities straight and to know we are progressing on the straight path, though the pace seems slow. In the Joseph Smith Translation of Matthew 6:33, notice both the focus and the promise: "Wherefore, *seek not the things of this world* but seek ye first *to build up* the kingdom of God, and *to establish his righteousness*; and all these things shall be added unto you." (JST, Matthew 6:38. Italics added.) Are we not grateful that it is He who decides which things of this world can safely "be added"?

If we think about it at all, the spiritual stimulants needed to keep us going have been prescribed for us by the Lord: feasting on the scriptures, serving others, praying, being reminded of our covenants by ordinances, and avoiding evil.

"Keeping at it" is a test not only of our faith, but also of our obedience. Furthermore, each gospel requirement, like missionary work, carries within itself its own witness that it is true and is its own renewal and refreshment. (D&C 84:80.) Then why, at times, does it seem that despite diligence, the renewal and the refreshment do not come precisely as expected by us? A few causes deserve special comment.

First, we forget that while we work *with* others, we are working *for* Him! Working for "them" can be very wearying. Our naive insistence on seeing rapid results —perhaps even undesired results—is intensified when we work for "them"; our expectations become unrealistic and, therefore, are not fulfilled. This weariness is of our own making, real as it is. But when we truly work for *Him* rather than for *others*, we will be less cluttered, less frantic—and more effective. We will also actually be more helpful to "them."

Second, in Jacob's extensive quotations from the prophet Zenos pertaining to the tame and wild trees, Israel and the Gentiles, there is ancillary wisdom about balance. The principles of pruning mentioned therein could be applied to how unpruned things can get out of hand, how clutter and excesses can sometimes accumulate in our lives.

We read about how, when they are unmanaged, "the branches thereof overcome the roots" by growing "faster than the strength of the roots, taking strength unto themselves." (Jacob 5:48.) The branches of our various time commitments can prove excessive if we are not careful.

The Lord desires a balance in which "the root and the top [are] equal in strength." (Jacob 5:66.) Such trees, in addition to enduring, will stand both heat and storm and will be productive. As the root system expands and deepens, more branches can be sustained.

Third, we forget that our time is actually His time; all our time is borrowed time. You and I have never met anyone who, with certainty, owned a week or a month, though we have met many who have thought they did. Often when we have given to Him, almost condescendingly, what time we choose to allocate, we unwisely declare our part of the transaction concluded. Do we really wish Him who gives us breath from moment to moment to declare His part concluded too? Besides, is there really something else we are to be doing with our lives that supersedes the importance of His work? Of course, things are to be done in wisdom and in order and with diligence. Of course, respite, renewal, and refreshment are vital. The Lord would not deny us these. Indeed, He has counseled us to see that we receive them. But, in ways known best to Him, He will insist on our overcoming the mistaken feeling that we own ourselves or our time. On judgment day, will some press their title to an acre in downtown Dallas when they stand before the Creator who has correctly called this world His footstool? Can we not spare an hour presently for Him who continues to spare us?

Can we, for instance, desire to follow Him, but only if it involves two or three hours a week? Can we truly desire to believe in Him if we are not also willing to be trained by Him? And how can training occur except "in process of time"?

Things go best when we remember that He has purchased us; we are His, our time and all else!

Fourth, we do not allow sufficiently for the agency of others. He has done so, and so must we. Their agency is just as precious as is our own. Often our desire for results takes no account of the agency of others, causing unnecessary weariness and frustration. Remembering how the Lord has structured this second estate with great preeminence given to freedom will help us to avoid this source of fatigue even when so many mortals expand so much energy trying to give away the precious freedom God gave them.

Fifth, we forget to pace ourselves at times. Rest and renewal permit us to go farther faster in this mortal marathon.

Sixth, we allow ourselves to get diverted not only from eternal objectives, but also into tasks that are not actually ours to do. This insightful case is instructive: "Then the twelve called the multitude of the disciples unto them, and said, It is not reason that we should leave the word of God, and serve tables." (Acts 6:2.)

The Twelve, had they not been inspired, could have easily ended up being very busy as regional welfare administrators and never left Jerusalem! There would have been plenty to do—many widows to be cared for. The Twelve, of course, realized that they had not been called to serve tables but, rather, to spread the word of God about the earth. Hence, they wisely delegated the welfare task to others. So the needs of the Greek widows—which were real—were met, but without sacrificing the Twelve's higher calling.

Sometimes in the Church we gravitate toward conspicuous busyness rather than doing what we have really been called to do. Getting thus diverted usually occurs, however, because of bad judgment rather than bad motives. When we fail to accord priority to our real opportunities, we tend to make Martha-like choices instead of Mary-like choices. Remember, it was Martha rather than Mary who "was cumbered." (Luke 10:40-42.)

A bishop who is merely a manager of programs or activities will be more weary and less effective than a bishop who is a shepherd of the flock. Doing those basic things we are supposed to be doing can permit us to proceed with confidence and in patience. Otherwise, indiscriminate busyness will result in trying to do too many things simultaneously, pursuing quickie campaigns and producing only temporary results at best.

Seventh, sometimes when we do not continue as we commenced, one reason is that sometimes we have commenced too much! When we have not counted the cost beforehand, there are overruns—emotionally and physically as well as financially.

"And whosoever doth not bear his cross, and come after me, cannot be my disciple. For which of you, intending to build a tower, sitteth not down first, and counteth the cost, whether he have sufficient to finish it? Lest haply, after he hath laid the foundation, and is not able to finish it, all that behold it begin to mock him, saying, This man began to build, and was not able to finish." (Luke 14:27-30.)

Eighth, often in the confusion of means and ends, we fail to see that programs and activities are helps, not ends in themselves, so far as developing the eternal attributes and everlasting skills are concerned. The character that can be developed by Scouting will be there in the next world, long after one has any need to make fire without matches.

Ninth, we often remain on plateaus of weariness because we rush from quickly *identifying* a problem to *implementing* a solution when, in fact, we should have spent time more wisely *identifying* the true nature of the challenge, then *developing prescriptions* to meet the challenge, and then *implementing* and *refining* our response to the challenge. Just as some people lose the same twenty pounds of weight every year, so some of us are always solving the same problem—over and over again. How weary one can get just running in place!

In any event, the Lord, through different prophets, has repeated for us the same needed counsel. Note these words of Paul: "And let us not be weary in well doing: for in due season we shall reap, if we faint not." (Galatians 6:9.) "But ye, brethren, be not weary in well doing." (2 Thessalonians 3:13.) Our bodies can be renewed and our minds can be free of weariness; it is a promise! (D&C 84:33, 80.) When we sing these lyrics we are reminding ourselves of some good counsel:

If the way be full of trial; Weary not!
If it's one of sore denial, Weary not!

If the way be one of sorrow, Weary not! . . .
Here we suffer tribulation,
Here we must endure temptation;
But there'll come a great salvation—Weary not!

If misfortune overtake us, Weary not!
Jesus never will forsake us, Weary not!
He will leave us never, never;
From His love there's naught can sever;
Glory to the Lamb forever!—Weary not!

Do not weary by the way,
Whatever be thy lot;
There awaits a brighter day . . .
To all, to all who weary not![63]

We need not be perpetual motion machines—merely forward motion machines. As George MacDonald said, "Work is not always required of a man. There is such a thing as a sacred idleness, the cultivation of which is now fearfully neglected."[64]

Without knowing that we are here on His errand, oh, how weary we could become living on without purpose on a pointless planet! It is this very weariness that is being experienced by many but is wisely commented on by only a few:

On the other hand, if buses and newspaper headlines and the man winding up clockwork pigs, all that happens, represent the whole significance of life, it is equally intolerable. For what does happen? I look backwards and see for individuals and societies a round as monotonous as the seasons of rising and falling hopes; I look forward and see the same process continuing; I look into my own heart and see such a tangle of desires, such fluctuating moods, such a burning passionate egotism, that, imagine my life as I will, I know it can yield no more than momentary satisfaction.[65]

However, once we align ourselves with God's purposes, then routine and the ordinary play their part, as John M. Synge said: "When men lose their poetic feeling for ordinary life, and cannot write of ordinary things, their exalted poetry is likely to lose its strength of exaltation in the way men cease to build beautiful churches when they have lost happiness in building shops."

Instead, disciples can have enough confidence in His cause so that most causes of weariness can be avoided and the unavoidable weariness can be absorbed. The throbbing assurances of prophecies such as this one from President John Taylor can lift us and spur us on:

This Church fail? No! Times and seasons may change, revolution may succeed revolution; thrones may be cast down; and empires be dissolved; earthquakes may rend the earth from center to circumference; and mountains may be hurled out of their places; and the mighty ocean be moved from its bed, but amidst the crash of worlds and the crack of matter, truth, eternal truth, must remain unchanged, and those principles which God has revealed to His saints be unscathed amidst the warring elements, and remain as firm as the throne of Jehovah.[66]

Someday, as William Law said, we shall see things much more clearly and our perspective will be eternal. "As the fixed stars, by reason of our being placed at such distance from them, appear but so many points; so when we, placed in eternity, shall look back on all time, it will all appear but as a moment. Then, a luxury, an indulgence, a prosperity, a greatness of fifty years will seem to every one that looks back on it as . . . short enjoyment."[67]

"Unwearied diligence" during this small moment of mortality with its seeming routine will enrich eternity far more than we know.

Chapter Seven

"Endure Well to the End"
(D&C 121:8)

Once we have become grounded, rooted, established, and settled, the concluding quality needed is to
endure well to the end. Clearly this is much more than
merely surviving over the months and the years of life:
"And then, if thou endure it *well*, God shall exalt thee
on high; thou shalt triumph over all thy foes." (D&C
121:8. Italics added.)

Patient perseverance in Christian service is part of
this final challenge: "To them who by patient continu-
ance in well doing seek for glory and honour and
immortality, eternal life." (Romans 2:7.) Commandment keeping, serving well, letting "all these things"
tutor us and give us that experience which is for our
good—these are things that should continue to the
end. We do not, therefore, merely go on living in the
world—we overcome it: "He that is faithful and
endureth shall overcome the world." (D&C 63:47.)

This means both developing the eternal qualities
needed and resisting temptations that continue in one
form or another to the very end. At the Last Supper,
Jesus commended His disciples, saying, "Ye are they

which have continued with me in my temptations."
(Luke 22:28.) Likewise, He will continue with us in our
temptations to the very end; even if in the matured disciple the temptation is no more than peevishness over
poor health, this too must be endured well.

The seeming ordinariness of life contains sufficient
growth challenges for us all and in all seasons of life.
Aging may remove some temptations but heighten
others; it may lessen the desire for preeminence such
as flourished during an aggressive earlier career, but it
may cause the growth of grumpiness later on.

So much of enduring means coping successfully
when confronted with customized chastening. "If ye
endure chastening, God dealeth with you as with
sons; for what son is he whom the father chasteneth
not? . . . Now *no chastening for the present seemeth to be
joyous, but grievous:* nevertheless *afterward it yieldeth* the
peaceable fruit of righteousness unto them which are
exercised thereby." (Hebrews 12:7, 11. Italics added.)

Paul's observations about how chastening at the
time is no pleasure or joy should put us on guard
against the naive notion that chastening "will be a
snap," producing no more than a ruffle in our emotions. God knows what must be done by way of our re-
finement, and the pain is apt to be precise and felt
where and when we are least ready to receive it.

Enduring *tribulation* increases our usefulness to
Him, "here and now" as well as "there and then": "For
verily I say unto you, blessed is he that keepeth my
commandments, whether in life or in death; and he
that is faithful in tribulation, the reward of the same is
greater in the kingdom of heaven." (D&C 58:2.)

Enduring also suggests not giving in, but holding
out. Indeed, the Lord even uses the words "hold out":
"If thou wilt do good, yea, and *hold out* faithful to the

115

end, thou shalt be saved in the kingdom of God." (D&C 6:13. Italics added.) He would not use words like "hold out" if the risks were not so real that we might "give in."

The accumulating experiences of life, including those incident to age, bring a subtle realization of something we have understood well—in theory—and that we have seen a hundred times in others: Trials come to *us*. We never really thought of ourselves as an exception, for such would be unrealistic, yet neither did we quite think this would happen to us and especially in this way!

We may not get angry with God, but sometimes we let Him know we are miffed. And if others will listen, we murmur to them as if to register with someone our discovery that we are not exceptions after all. Exceptional souls are not developed, however, by being made exceptions to the challenges that are common to mankind.

Enduring even includes the irony in which the worthy suffer for righteousness' sake: "Blessed are they which are persecuted *for righteousness' sake*: for theirs is the kingdom of heaven." (Matthew 5:10. Italics added.) And as for these times of terrorism, this counsel is given: "But and if ye suffer for righteousness' sake, happy are ye: and *be not afraid of their terror*, neither be troubled." (1 Peter 3:14. Italics added.)

Since "persecution ariseth because of the word," and since some then become offended (Matthew 13:21), enduring the indignity of being wronged for being right is yet another irony.

Being misunderstood even when engaged in well-doing is part of it, too: "For it is better, if the will of God be so, that ye suffer for well doing, than for evil doing." (1 Peter 3:17.)

Suffering for the name of Christ and as a Christian, centuries ago, once so very real and widespread a thing, is a challenge that will now be sharpened again, and by more than secularism alone. These verses will come to have fresh meaning all over again:

"If ye be reproached for the name of Christ, happy are ye; for the spirit of glory and of God resteth upon you: on their part he is evil spoken of, but on your part he is glorified.

"Yet if any man suffer as a Christian, let him not be ashamed; but let him glorify God on his behalf." (1 Peter 4:14, 16.)

For Latter-day Saints, the double irony will be to suffer abuse from some who claim we are not Christians and, at the same time, from others precisely because we are! Such can do wonderful things to concentrate our commitments. Was Jesus not persecuted both *for not being* the political Savior some Jews expected, and, at the same time, *for being* a threat to the political order?

As we endure a tiny fraction of what He endured, we come to know the "fellowship of his sufferings." (Philippians 3:10.) It is the most exclusive fraternity, and the dues are high.

Thus enduring is not simply a passive absorption of trials; rather, it is an activism that affirms not only one's faith, but also the basic joy of life!

In all of this, therefore, we cannot expect to be spared our equivalent of what Saints in other ages have endured. What the Lord has said of His people previously is true currently: "Nevertheless the Lord seeth fit to chasten his people; yea, he trieth their patience and their faith." (Mosiah 23:21.) "My people must be tried in all things, that they may be prepared to receive the glory that I have for them, even the glory of Zion; and he that will not bear chastisement is not worthy of my kingdom." (D&C 136:31.) And the Lord does all this so extraordinarily well in the midst of our seemingly ordinary lives.

With chastisement comes the chance for improvement, which, though we do not welcome it, we at least do not reject and resent it. Chastisement may occur in the most private circumstances of life or quite publicly. Either way, it is usually a major challenge for our egos. To be dressed down, as it were, just when we are dressed up, appearing to be something other than we are, is no small blow. Do we really love light enough "to be made glad"—even when we are shown to be wrong, when we thought "others were wrong"?[68] Can we still take reproof when what others say is essentially correct but is said poorly and insensitively—or even with the wrong motives on their part? Are we willing to be held back a grade in the school of life while our contemporaries move on—until we get a certain lesson through our heads? Our Headmaster will not hesitate to do that, if necessary.

Properly responded to, temptation, persecution, and tribulation can do wonderful things to refine our lives. Perhaps it is only when the things that do not matter are made to fall away that we see, at last, "things as they really are"! Then the worries of the world soon disappear from one's "radarscope":

> Now, the prospect of death overshadows all others. I am like a man on a sea voyage nearing his destination. When I embarked I worried about having a cabin with a porthole, whether I should be asked to sit at the captain's table, who were the more attractive and important passengers. All such considerations become pointless when I shall soon be disembarking.[69]

Being settled and established contributes much to assist us in achieving a paced diligence. An unrooted soul is especially vulnerable, because, superficially, he may have done what was asked for, but, apparently, has not been given the promised blessing. No matter that the approach was in error; time was given and energy expended. Why not, therefore, "chuck it"? It is one of Lucifer's oldest ploys, and, unfortunately, it still works. Contrariwise, when rooted, one has some sense about the seasons of life and about planting and nurturing before expecting the harvest. "Phase one" disciples do not yet understand about the seasons that go with seasoning of a soul.

As we endure well, the Lord will also help us to pick ourselves up after our tumbles. He will help to heal our bruises. He will even help us wash away the dirt and the grime. Finally, even the memories of the wrong that we have done will be gone. For if we are truly repentant His promise is: "Come now, and let us reason together, saith the Lord: though your sins be as scarlet, they shall be as white as snow; though they be red like crimson, they shall be as wool." (Isaiah 1:18.)

But enduring the requirements of repentance involves so much more than just a weekend of sorrow; scarlet stain does not fade away quite so easily. Our forgiving Lord will not even mention our poor past, if we endure in true repentance:

"But if the wicked will turn from all his sins that he hath committed, and keep all my statutes, and do that which is lawful and right . . . All his transgressions that he hath committed, they shall *not be mentioned unto him:* in his righteousness that he hath done he shall live." (Ezekiel 18:21-22. Italics added.)

God's grace will be sufficient for us whatever our stage of spiritual maturity in the midst of temptation, persecution, tribulation, and even seeming deprivation, for He is the true Tutor pacing His pupils:

"Behold, ye are little children and ye cannot bear all things now; ye must grow in grace and in the knowledge of the truth." (D&C 50:40.)

Grace is God's favor, help, or gift that comes to us according to our needs and our personal righteousness. So it is, when we feel inadequate, if we are humble and weak, that His grace is sufficient for us.

"And when I had said this, the Lord spake unto me, saying: Fools mock, but they shall mourn; and *my grace is sufficient for the meek*, that they shall take no advantage of your weakness;

"And if men come unto me *I will show unto them their weakness*. I give unto men weakness that they may be humble; and my grace is sufficient for all men that humble themselves before me; for if they humble themselves before me, and have faith in me, then will I *make weak things become strong unto them*." (Ether 12:26-27. Italics added.)

If we were not serious about our submissiveness to Him, could we endure having our weaknesses shown to us? And if we did not love Him, could we trust Him enough to be patiently tutored by Him until the very weakness becomes a strength?

As long as a particular period in our life might seem to us, this brief mortal experience does pass so quickly; this is no small consideration when we are talking of enduring. Mortality is but a moment.

Ironically, time and life pass even faster when we are happy. Enduring is made so much easier, too, when we are growing. We can, as Alma said, even sense our growth and the enlargement of our soul, and can say within ourselves, "This is a good seed" and this is a good life! (Alma 32:28.)

The Church, along with offering authority, ordinances, organization, and doctrine, aids us in so many ways as we grow. It reminds us of our need for service to others and provides us opportunities for service. It reminds us of our need to study the scriptures and provides us opportunities to study the scriptures. It presents opportunities to be taught and opportunities to teach. It provides opportunities to both lead and be led. The Church causes us, as it were, to set aside time and space in our busy schedule in order to provide much of the growth curriculum for the laboratory of life. But it also provides us with encouragement and counsel to ensure periods of respite, renewal, and refreshment. The following scripture is far more instructive in this regard than a casual reading suggests:

"And the apostles gathered themselves together unto Jesus, and told him all things, both what they had done, and what they had taught.

"And he said unto them, *Come ye yourselves apart* into a desert place, and *rest a while*: for there were many coming and going, and they had *no leisure* so much as to eat.

"And they departed into a desert place by ship *privately*." (Mark 6:30-32. Italics added.)

We rest and have some solitude in order to better serve those who may contribute to our fatigue!

Even with respite and pace, as George MacDonald said, life nevertheless seems to come "flowing over [us] from behind."[70] However, the fact that we are sometimes surprised by the sudden surf of circumstances does not mean that what flows over us "from behind" is disordered at all. Were He to let us see too much of the future, we would surely neglect some of the present, looking beyond present challenges—sometimes with anticipation and other times with intimidation—to those things yet future.

The holy present does deserve our best. Even its

enjoyment could be dampened by our foreseeing too clearly an impending deprivation, a loss of a loved one, a new cross waiting to be shouldered. Would it really be helpful to a family vacation to know ahead of time that it would be the last that one's health would permit? Those things which are on both sides just beyond the veil, except on His terms, cannot be allowed to press in too much on this estate.

Being generally confined to *now*, with each *now* being part of that which happens "in process of time," fits snugly with yet another reality: While we are to be full of mercy and empathy and to share the sorrows and burdens of others, the neighbor's burdens at a particular point will become *his*, just as Jesus' incalculable burdens became His. We assist others in the carrying of their crosses, but, finally, their crosses are theirs, and ours are *ours*. When a child dies, neighbors can console and even try to understand, but the parents must bear that special sorrow which is exclusively theirs.

The physical pain of another can be sensed but not really felt. In similar ways, recalling some of one's own past physical pain is not easy. We remember that the pain was bad, perhaps even very bad. We remember some of the things we did in reaction to that pain. But we cannot really feel that pain *now*, retroactively. Mercifully, the present is the present—not the past. Only *He* bore the burden of past, present, and future pain at the same time!

Only *He* can understand perfectly and feel fully that which we endure by way of pains, afflictions, and temptations of every kind. How? Because, long ago, He took upon Himself not only our sins, but also our very infirmities "and the sicknesses of his people." (Alma 7:11-12.)

Without the trial of Gethsemane and Calvary and the assumption of all our sins, sicknesses, afflictions, and infirmities, as George MacDonald has observed, "The temptations of our Master [would] not be so full as the human cup could hold; there would have been one region through which we had to pass wherein we might call aloud upon our Captain-Brother, and there would have been no voice or hearing: He had avoided the fatal spot!"[71]

But because Jesus bore the full weight of the sins and afflictions of the human family, descending below all, His empathy is perfect!

We need have no reluctance about communications with Him. One trembles at the realization, therefore, that our own empathy is likewise not technique alone, but is shared substance, too. Will we, therefore, willingly undergo some experiences in order to help us to better understand others?

Thus it is that the everlasting skill of communicating is tied to our experience and to the resulting empathy.

Annie Sophie Swetchine said, "Those who have suffered much are like those who know many languages; they have learned to understand and be understood by all." So Jesus by His suffering was made perfect in His understanding!

The sufferers are sensitive to the differing ways in which God communicates with us. "God whispers to us in our pleasures, speaks in our conscience, but shouts in our pains: it is His megaphone to rouse a deaf world."[72]

As we strive to endure well to the very end, the fact is that the proving purposes of this life must ever be a part of our awareness as to what is really underway. Furthermore, we must face the reality that *proving* is a *process* as well as a *purpose.* There will surely be stressful moments when, unwisely, we will momentarily wish otherwise: the seemingly relentless and repetitive chores continue when a little respite is so much desired; a new lesson to be learned is thrust upon us when we have barely finished the last lesson and had hoped for a reflective recess; certain remedial work must be done again, calling into question our very capacity to develop more fully a certain elusive attribute; a re-extrusion of ego occurs just when we thought a tendency had been finally overcome; diversions and incursions continue to draw us away from what seems to be our real work; and an unintended and unhelpful sense of isolation develops amid our challenges because of the insensitivities of others to our needs.

But the finishing and polishing process continues —and so must enduring. Therefore, as with Him, it is finished only when we are finished, and it is as shaped and finished as we are willing to become before we, too, reach the end of that portion of His work that He has given us to do. (John 19:30.)

Footnotes

[1]Brigham Young, *Discourses of Brigham Young* (Salt Lake City: Deseret Book, 1977), p. 12. Italics added.

[2]Joseph F. Smith, *Conference Report*, April 1912, p. 5.

[3]As told by Brigham Young in general conference, October 7, 1860. *Journal of Discourses* 8:198.

[4]Walter Bagehot, *The Works of Walter Bagehot*, ed. Forrest Morgan (Hartford, Conn.: The Travelers Insurance Company, 1889), 1:100.

[5]John A. Widtsoe, *Evidences and Reconciliations* (Salt Lake City: Bookcraft, 1960), p. 226.

[6]Brigham Young, January 12, 1862, *Journal of Discourses* 9:150. Italics added.

[7]Brigham Young, October 7, 1859, *Journal of Discourses* 7:277. Italics added.

[8]Boyd K. Packer, address given at welfare session of general conference, April 1, 1978, *Ensign*, May 1978, p. 92.

[9]Malcolm Muggeridge, in *William F. Buckley, Jr., and Malcolm Muggeridge on Faith and Religious Institutions* (New York: The National Committee of Catholic Laymen, Inc., 1981), p. 5.

[10]*The Works of Walter Bagehot* 2:313.

[11]C. S. Lewis, ed., *George MacDonald: An Anthology* (New York: Macmillan Publishing Co., 1974), p. 144.

[12]Buckley and Muggeridge, p. 6.

[13]*History of the Church* 4:162-64. Quoted in an address delivered by Elder Boyd K. Packer at the Fifth Annual Church Educational System Religious Educators Symposium, August 12, 1981, Brigham Young University. *BYU Studies*, Summer 1981, pp. 259-78.

[14]Edward Norman, *Christianity and the World Order* (Oxford: Oxford University Press, 1979), p. 77.

[15]Roy W. Doxey, *The Doctrine and Covenants Speaks 2* (Salt Lake City: Deseret Book, 1979): 130.

[16]John Taylor, *The Government of God* (Liverpool: S. W. Richards, 1852), p. 53.

[17]As quoted in Roy W. Doxey, *Latter-day Prophets and the Doctrine and Covenants* 1 (Salt Lake City: Deseret Book, 1963): 22.

[18]George Will, *The Pursuit of Happiness, and Other Sobering Thoughts* (New York: Harper & Row, 1978), p. 228.

[19]G. K. Chesterton, *All Things Considered* (Henley on Thames, England: Darwin Finlayson Ltd., 1969), pp. 142-43.

[20]*The Works of Walter Bagehot* 2:319.

[21]Malcolm Muggeridge, *Things Past*, ed. Ian Hunter (New York: William Morrow, 1979), p. 249.

[22]*The Works of Walter Bagehot* 2:311.

[23]Ibid., 2:48.

[24]Alexander Solzhenitsyn, *Warning to the West* (New York: Farrar, Straus and Giroux, 1976), p. 79.

[25]C. S. Lewis, *The Weight of Glory* (Grand Rapids, Mich.: William B. Eerdmans, 1965), pp. 44-45.

[26]Richard Hoftstadter, *Academic Freedom in the Age of the College* (New York: Columbia University Press, 1955), p. 6.

[27]Ibid., p. 83.

[28]Perry Miller, *The New England Mind: The Seventeenth Century* (Boston: Beacon Press, 1954), p. 82. Italics in original.

[29]Ibid., p. 84.

[30]Leo Tolstoy, *Essays, Letters, Misc.* 2 (Thomas Y. Crowell, 1899): 98.

[31]William J. Bennett, "Getting Ethics," *Commentary*, December 1980, p. 65.

[32]Mark W. Cannon, Administrative Assistant to the Chief Justice of the United States, in an address to the Southwestern Judicial Conference, Santa Fe, New Mexico, June 4, 1981.

[33]Robert H. Horwitz, *The Moral Foundations of the American Republic*, 2nd ed. (Charlottesville: University Press of Virginia, 1979), p. 166.

[34]Ortega y Gasset, J., *The Modern Theme* (New York: Harper & Row, 1961), as quoted in Duncan William, *Trousered Apes* (New Rochelle, N.Y.: Arlington House, 1971), p. 69.

[35]*The Dunciad*, book IV.

[36]*George MacDonald: An Anthology*, p. 80.

[37]From the *Common School Journal*, 1841, as quoted in Joy Elmer Morgan, *Horace Mann: His Ideas and Ideals* (Washington, D.C.: National Home Library Foundation, 1936), p. 133.

[38]Seymour Y. Glick, "Humanistic Medicine in a Modern Age," *New England Journal of Medicine*, April 23, 1981, p. 1037.

[39]Alexis de Tocqueville, "Democracy in America," as quoted in Andrew M. Scott, *Political Thought in America* (New York: Holt, Rinehart and Winston, 1965), p. 225.

[40]As quoted in *A College-Related Church: United Methodist Perspectives*, (The National Commission on United Methodist Higher Education), p. 17.

[41]As quoted in *Trousered Apes*, p. 143.

[42]Charles W. Penrose, *Conference Report*, October 1911, p. 48.

[43]*The Works of Walter Bagehot* 1:42.

[44]Ibid., 2:302.

[45]*George MacDonald: An Anthology*, p. 33.

[46]G. K. Chesterton, *St. Francis of Assisi* (London: Hodder & Stoughton Ltd., 1923), p. 24.

[47]M. J. Sobran, "In Loco Parentis," *The Human Life Review*, Fall 1979, p. 12.

[48]*George MacDonald: An Anthology*, p. 24.

[49]Will Durant, *The Story of Civilization*, vol. 3: *Caesar and Christ* (New York: Simon and Schuster, 1944), p. 667.

[50]Aaron Stern, *Me—The Narcissistic American* (New York: Ballantine Books, 1979). As quoted in Roger J. Bulger, "Narcissus, Pogo, and Lew Thomas' Wager," *Journal of the American Medical Association*, April 10, 1981, p. 1450.

[51]Arianna Stassinopoulous, "The Inflation of Politics and the Disintegration of Culture," *Imprimis* 7, no. 3 (March 1978), p. 5.

[52]Michael Novak, "The Family Out of Favor," *Harper's*, April 1976, p. 44.

[53]Alberta Siegel, "The Effects of Media Violence on Social Learning," in *Violence and the Media: A Staff Report to the National Commission on the Causes of Violence* (Washington, D.C.: U.S. Government Printing Office, 1969), p. 279.

[54]Winston Churchill, Address, Harrow School, October 29, 1941.

[55]Harold B. Lee, *Conference Report*, October 1951, pp. 26-27.

[56]James E. Talmage, *Jesus the Christ* (Salt Lake City: Deseret Book, 1973), p. 579; Matthew 15:5-6, 20-21.

[57]*George MacDonald: An Anthology*, p. 3. Italics added.

[58]Ibid., p. 153. Italics in original.

[59]Ibid., p. 37.

[60]William Law, *A Serious Call to a Devout and Holy Life* (Grand Rapids, Mich.: Sovereign Grace Publishers, 1971), p. 114.

[61]Ibid., p. 162.

[62]Penelope Fitzgerald, *The Knox Brothers* (New York: Coward, McCann & Geoghegan, Inc., 1977), p. 29.

[63]"If the Way Be Full of Trial, Weary Not," Deseret Sunday School Songs, 1909, no. 158. Words by W. H. Flaville; music by John R. Sweeney.

[64]*George MacDonald: An Anthology*, p. 123.

[65]Malcolm Muggeridge, *Things Past*, p. 74.

[66]*Times and Seasons*, December 15, 1844, 5:744.

[67]*A Serious Call to a Devout and Holy Life*, p. 78.

[68]*George MacDonald: An Anthology*, p. 102.

[69]Malcolm Muggeridge,*Things Past*.

[70]*George MacDonald: An Anthology*, p. 134.

[71]Ibid., pp. 15-16.

[72]C. S. Lewis, *The Problem of Pain* (New York: The Macmillan Company, 1962), p. 93.

Index

Repentance, 4, 47-48, 119
Resentment toward Zion, 17-18
Reynolds, Edward, 82
Revelation, 19-23
Riches, danger of, 5, 24
Righteousness, 5, 75
Rights, selfish, 26, 31-32
Rome, examples of, 93
Rooted, being, 15, 31, 88
Root system, 17-18, 26, 108
Rutherford, Ernest, 64

Sadness, sources of, 38
Salvation, plan of. *See* Plan of
    salvation
Satan, 44-45, 93-94
Savior. *See* Jesus Christ
Schooling process, mortal: results
    of, 6-7; as curriculum, 13, 35-37,
    67; involves Headmaster or Tutor,
    35-36, 118
Scorching, effects of, 31
Second coming. *See* Summer
    (preceding second coming)
Second estate: characteristics of, 3-5;
    led through, 10; structure of, 11,
    35; features lessons, 14; free
    agency is part of, 36; acceptance
    of, 36-37; experiences unique to, 47
Secularism, 79, 86-87, 95-96
Security, 24-25
Seed, gospel, 16-17
Selfishness, 31-32, 92, 94-95
Self-reliance: righteous, 19-22;
    unrighteous, 80
Settled, being: in our discipleship,
    12-13; aspects of, 12-13; in
    devotion to Savior, 15; meaning
    of, 18; spiritually, 19, 32; requires
    use of Holy Spirit, 22-23; helps
    our perspective, 25-26;
    accelerating, 32; permanence,
    32-34; process of, 51-52; evidence
    of, 63
Siegel, Alberta, 95
Silvester, David, 33-34
Sin, 24-26
Skills, everlasting, 11, 66-67, 74-76.
    See also Attributes, eternal
Smith, George A., 21
Smith, Joseph, 47-49, 80
Smith, Joseph F., 19-20
Sobran, Joseph, 90

Solzhenitsyn, Alexander, 80-81
Son of Man. *See* Jesus Christ
Song, Deseret Sunday School, 112
Spiritual maturity, 18-19, 33, 47-49
Stassinopoulous, Arianna, 95
Stern, Aaron, 93
Submission to the Lord, 7, 61-63, 77
Suffering, 7-8
Summer (preceding second coming):
    as climax of mortal time, 17;
    characteristics of, 19, 59-60, 78-81,
    97-99; education as an example
    of, 81-90; as related to parable of
    the Ten Virgins, 97-99; as related
    to parable of the Sower, 98-99
Swetchine, Annie Sophie, 123
Synge, John M., 113

Talmage, James E., 98-99
Taylor, John, 58, 113
Temptations, 11, 24-27, 40-46
Third estate, 61
Time: measured to man, 10; no
    more, 11; experiences in process
    of, 24; learning in process of,
    30-31, 47, 49-51; passage of, 31,
    120; balancing of, spent, 32;
    misuse of, 70; is the Lord's time,
    108-9; to plan, 111; present, 121-22
Tocqueville, Alexis de, 85-86
Tolstoy, Leo, 83
Trials and tribulations: view of, in
    the future, 27-29; enduring, 39-41,
    115-18; God's promises
    concerning, 43; no immunity from,
    45; as refining process, 118
Truth, 80, 82, 84-89

Universities, 82-83
Uriah, 71-72

Veil, 3-4, 37

Washington, George, 84
Weariness: from physical fatigue,
    100; relief from, 102; often
    self-induced, 103; causes of, 104-9;
    nine areas to watch for in, 107-12;
    avoiding and absorbing, 113
Widtsoe, John A., 21
World, 37-38

Young, Brigham, 19, 21-22, 52-53